THE ALL WHITES

A History of Newton Abbot Rugby Club 1873–2013

Major John Evans DSO & Michael Bennie

ALL WHITES

NEWTON ABBOT
RFC

HALSGROVE

First published in Great Britain in 2014
Copyright © John Evans 2014
additional material © Michael Bennie 2014
photographs © NARFC or individual owners 2014

PUBLISHER'S NOTE

The years in which historic photographs were taken is added where known.
Photos taken in the modern era appear chronologically or are grouped relating
to various events, competitions and teams.

A CIP record for this title is available from the British Library

ISBN 978 0 85704 220 0

HALSGROVE
Halsgrove House,
Ryelands Business Park,
Bagley Road, Wellington, Somerset TA21 9PZ
Tel: 01823 653777   Fax: 01823 216796
email: sales@halsgrove.com

Part of the Halsgrove group of companies.
Information on all Halsgrove titles is available at: www.halsgrove.com

Printed and bound in China by Everbest Printing Co Ltd

Major John Evans, DSO

Acknowledgements

By Graham Rooke, FCA, Club President

NEWTON ABBOT RUGBY FOOTBALL CLUB, the authors and the current club committee would like to acknowledge the contributions of a great many people in the preparation of this history.

Some have given much valuable time as volunteers and some have given donations of money over the period since Major Evans wrote the first draft of his account the first 100 years of the club. There are too many of you to mention by name, but you know who you are, and I would like to thank you on behalf of us all.

I ceased to be Club Chairman in 2012, but I would particularly like to thank Mike Brooks, our current Club Secretary, without whose time and effort this publication might still not have come to fruition.

As the newly elected President of the Club, I am especially pleased that, after all this time, the efforts of Major Evans have finally made it into print. Thank you for your patience, Major Evans.

Contents

Foreword   6
Introduction   7

THE PRE-WAR ERA

Chapter 1   'Would You Like a
Game of Football?'   11
Chapter 2   The Pioneer Years   14
Chapter 3   Overseas Visitors   18
Chapter 4   The Second Golden Age   20
Chapter 5   The 'Great Rugby Rumpus'   22
Chapter 6   The Third Golden Age   24
Chapter 7   The Pre-War Years   28
Chapter 8   The Return of the All Blacks   40

INTO THE NEW ERA

Chapter 9   Picking up the Pieces   45
Chapter 10   Rackerhayes   48
Chapter 11   The Passing of the Old Guard   51
Chapter 12   Controversy and Tragedy   53
Chapter 13   Ton Up!   56

THE MODERN ERA

Chapter 14   The Journey Continues   81

Appendix I   Office Holders   132
Appendix II   Merit Tie Recipients   135
Appendix III   Winners of Club Awards   136
Appendix IV   Representative Honours   141
Appendix V   500 Board   142
Appendix VI   Life Members, 2013   142
Appendix VII   1st XV Playing Record,
1884–1935   143
Appendix VIII   Leading Points Scorers,
1946–73   144

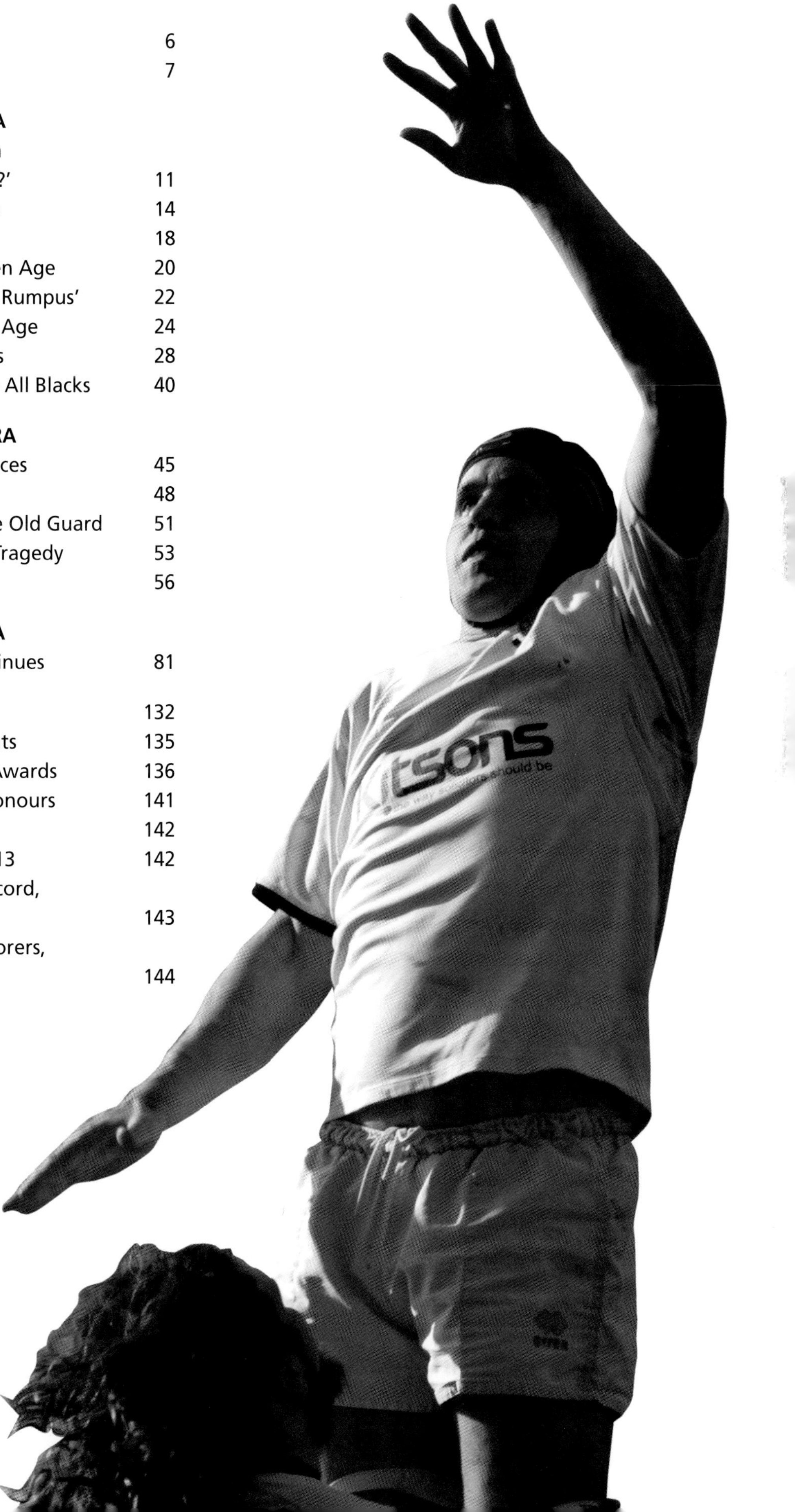

Foreword

By Scott Hastings

I FIRST VISITED the All Whites whilst the Rugby World Cup was taking place in Australia in 2003. At the time I was working with ITV on their coverage of the tournament and Russ Baker invited me down to a fundraiser for the boys who were going out to play in the Dubai Sevens. I have always enjoyed my time both on and off pitch and that night will long live in the memory! I even mentioned the club in my studio chat during the quarter final coverage following the dinner and have dined out on that story ever since!

Since then I have been impressed by the recent developments that I have seen at first hand. The All Whites are playing at their highest ever level; the new ladies and girls' teams, the huge number of children now playing rugby every week are a testament to its long history. The ongoing success of the club is dependent on the support of its sponsors and the good will and commitment of a small number of volunteers and parents who, over the years have made sure it all happens.

I am delighted to endorse this wonderful book with its vibrant memories of rugby over the years in South Devon and of how the club has overcome so many difficulties to become the powerful presence it is today.

I look forward to my next visit to the club, and wish you all the very best with the History of Newton Abbot Rugby Club.

Scott Hastings

Scott is Scotland's most capped center three quarter with 65 caps. He played in 51 Internationals with his brother Gavin and they are the only brothers to have played together in a British Lions Test match. A former captain and full-back with Scottish Schools, out of George Watson's College in Edinburgh, he was first capped for Scotland a month after his 21st birthday in January 1986 against France. Ever present in the Scotland team for a period of 11 years he captained the Barbarians against the 1993 All Blacks and Captained Scotland at 7 a-side rugby. He played in ten of Scotland's fourteen World Cup games in 1987, 1991, 1995 and joined ITV's commentary team for the 1999, 2003 and 2007 Rugby World Cups. In 1989 Scott played in 9 of the 11 games with the British and Irish Lions on their winning tour of Australia, including the final two test matches. He also toured with the Lions in 1993 on the tour to New Zealand but returned to the UK after 5 weeks having sustained a facial injury one week before the first test match.

Scott was a full time rugby player with the Scottish Rugby Union and Edinburgh Reivers for two years before retiring from professional rugby in January 1999. He retired from playing with his beloved Watsonians after 19 seasons and 227 games for the First XV in April 2002 but still retains a role with the club as their commercial and sponsorship director.

He is currently a freelance marketing and media consultant and undertakes numerous speaking engagements and motivational seminars for blue chip companies. For three years Scott was the main match commentator on Scottish Television's Rugby Roundup programme and covered his first International match between Scotland and the Barbarians in May 2001 for Channel 5. Scott continues to be involved in the media and writes the occasional newspaper column. He is also a regular commentator with Sky Sports in their coverage of the Heineken Cup and IRB7's and co-host of STV's Rugby highlights programme on the Magner's League. During the 6 Nations he commentates with the Irish channel, RTE.

Introduction

MAJOR JOHN EVANS, a past Chairman of Newton Abbot Rugby Football Club, and still today a strong supporter of the club, undertook extensive research into its history with a view to collecting it into a book to celebrate the club's centenary in 1973. Unfortunately, for a number of reasons, this book was not published at the time. Several attempts have since been made to revive the project without success, but following an approach to me by two Directors of the club, Mike Brooks and Graham Rooke, we are now able to see the fruits of his efforts.

This book is largely based on his researches into the first hundred years. I have simply added some background information in order to put the history of the club into the context of the development of rugby in general; additional material on the various visitors Newton has hosted; and a final chapter, based on information provided by current members of the club, giving a brief outline of developments in the last forty years. But it is in many ways a 'work in progress'. It has not been possible to provide the level of detail for the last forty years that Major Evans managed to achieve for the first hundred years, and the final chapter is therefore just a brief account of the main events and influences since 1973. It is, however, hoped that someone will be willing to undertake a similarly detailed labour of love covering the post-centenary years in time for the 150th anniversary in ten years' time. Anyone who has information that would help in this endeavour is therefore asked to contact the club.

The history of Newton Abbot Rugby Football Club can be seen as a journey – a journey that to a large extent mirrors the journey of rugby as a game, from the earliest days when standardised rules were still being formulated to today's highly organised structure. As with all journeys, there have been ups and downs, moments of glory and disappointment, times when the very existence of the club was under threat and only the dedication and community spirit of its members pulled it through. It has seen the club survive two World Wars and the loss of some of its most stalwart members and players – some in particularly poignant and tragic circumstances – and embrace a number of new initiatives, including in recent decades the introduction of the National League structure and the increasing importance of developmental work, with junior and mini sides.

The resilience the All Whites have shown in the lean times, and their ability to respond to new challenges in a constantly changing world, have brought them to their current position of strength, both on the playing field and off, and will no doubt stand them in good stead as they go forward. The journey continues.

Michael Bennie
Newton Abbot
June 2013

Major John Evans, centre, with former players

THE PRE-WAR ERA

CHAPTER 1

'Would You Like a Game of Football?'

IT ALL STARTED at the annual shooting match of the Newton Abbot Corps of the 10th Devon Rifles Volunteers in 1873. The Rev. George Townsend Warner of Newton College, an independent school in the town, who had formed a College team the year before, asked if the Volunteers would like a game. The answer was 'Yes', and the Newton Volunteers Club (sometimes referred to as the Newton Rifles) came into being. They adopted the Devon regimental colours of red and green in hoops as their club colours, and a playing field was laid out at Teign Marshes, which is now part of the Newton Abbot Racecourse car park. An entrance fee of 4d was introduced, later reduced to 3d.

Rugby football was still in its infancy. It is well known that the game originated at Rugby School, but not, as legend has it, with William Webb Ellis picking up the ball and running with it; it was more a process of evolution. Handling of the ball had long been common, although it was probably not until 1842 that players were allowed to run with it in their hands. Some of the pupils at the school produced a codified set of rules in 1845. However, different schools played by different rules – there was an Eton version of football, a Harrow version and several others besides Rugby's. This caused a certain amount of chaos when former pupils of the different schools tried to play together when they went up to university!

By 1860, however, many schools were playing by Rugby's rules, and clubs were being formed by their old boys. In 1863 the Football Association was formed and set about standardising the rules of the game. Some clubs, notably Blackheath, refused to join, however, and continued to play by Rugby rules. But there was still a degree of confusion, even within the Rugby form of the game, so in 1871, representatives of twenty-one clubs gathered to form the Rugby Football Union (RFU), thus formalising the name of the game and differentiating it irrevocably from Association Football or 'soccer'. In fact, it was not until 1888, fifteen years after the formation of the first rugby club, that the first game according to Association rules was played in Newton Abbot. The local newspaper commented: 'This seemed to afford little interest to those lovers of Rugby football who are accustomed to witnessing the dashing play of Newton Abbot's rugby representatives.'

The RFU set about standardising the rules to eliminate at least some of the confusion between different interpretations of the Rugby game. One of these rules was to outlaw hacking and tripping – which were apparently quite common in the earlier days – as some clubs refused to play any team that indulged in these practices.

However, this standardisation only went so far, and the game as played in the 1870s was very different from that of today. For example, there were originally no rules regarding team sizes or playing positions; although after the formation of the RFU, teams were restricted to a maximum of twenty. This was reduced in 1877 to fifteen, although in the 1879/80 season, Newton Volunteers only fielded fourteen players. Newton College's team also consisted of fourteen players: two backs, two three-quarter backs, two half backs and eight forwards. After 1880, however, fifteen became the norm, but sometimes with combinations of positions that seem strange today. For example, in one game teams consisted of a back, two three-quarter backs, two half backs and ten forwards. And in an inter-county game between Devon and Cornwall in 1885, Cornwall played one full back, three three-quarter backs, two half backs and nine forwards while Devon had two full backs and two three-quarters. The first time Newton played a team with present-day positions was in March 1888: Mapleton was full back, Paige (captain), Bearne, Newton and McDonald three-quarter backs, Challacombe and Taylor half backs, and Ball, Steer, Rise, Mills, Inch, Gardiner Scagell and Elliott. Their opponents, Tiverton, however, still had nine forwards and only three three-quarters.

The rules regarding scoring were also very different. Originally, only goals (dropped goals or converted tries) were counted; unconverted tries were only taken into account if the teams had scored an equal number of goals. This may have been due to the fact that in the first years of the game tries were something of a rarity – with twenty or more players in the opposing team, it was not easy to cross their line. Some clubs, including at one point Newton Abbot, also took into account 'minor points' (when a side touched the ball down behind its own try line) – and 'posters' (when a goal attempt hit the post). This form of scoring was shown in a match report on 1 March 1880:

> Plymouth elected to kick uphill (!), but many minutes elapsed before Bewes ran in behind the goal line, but being collared let go the ball, and a dispute arose as to whether he had fairly touched down the ball. We took our try, however, under protest, but failed to kick the goal. Liddell, for Plymouth, grounded the ball beneath our posts, from which a poster was kicked. Result: Newton 2 goals, 1 disputed try, Plymouth 1 goal, 1 poster.

In 1886, points were introduced for tries for the first time. A try was worth 1 point, while a goal (dropped or converted from a try) scored 3. The rules changed several more times during the 1880s and 1890s: in 1888 penalties were introduced, with a score of 2; in 1891 the values were increased, with a try worth 2, a penalty 3 and a goal 5; and in 1893 a try scored 3 points (although a converted try remained 5).

The rules did not originally include provision for officials. It was for the captains of the two teams to decide between them whether an offence had been committed. In 1875, umpires were introduced, but they were not mandatory – teams decided between themselves whether or not to have them. However, the presence of the umpires, who were appointed by the teams, did not entirely eliminate disputed results. For example, in December, in a match between Newton Rifles and Brixham Trawlers, 'the ball was touched down by Brixham, then picked up and moved forward a yard. The Brixham umpire said it was legal. The Newton umpire disagreed and Brixham walked off five minutes before time.'

Another incident was reported in the local press on 22 November 1882:

Totnes Wanderers touched down a disputed try and Newton gave way. Then the Totnes umpire, who was not standing behind the goal, also gave the conversion. This was hotly disputed by the Newton umpire, team and spectators. Totnes then walked off. Hutchings [the Newton captain] suggested that if the captain of Totnes could not keep command of his temper and learn courtesy he should not undertake to play again.

Bad sportsmanship is thus clearly not a modern phenomenon! Nor, it seems is 'football hooliganism'. In 1880, the Rev. Warner complained that the language of 'young Newton' at Newton College matches 'under stress of excitement' was extremely offensive to ladies and young boys, and proposed forming a Townsmen's Watch Committee to deal with any unruly elements at matches. And in a knock-out tournament in Exeter in April 1888, a group of Exeter spectators were guilty of 'blackguard behaviour' and rushed the field to prevent a conversion being taken. The Newton players 'got away safely from the mud throwing mob' although one of the officials, a Mr Davey was 'set upon and suffered grievously'. Indeed, games with Exeter were subsequently cancelled because of rough play and spectators' bad language. In 1898, the *Mid-Devon Advertiser* saw fit to publish a code for players:

Pluck, not brute force and ignorance, but play the game hard in a gentlemanly and sportsmanlike manner. Patience, an even temper, a silent tongue, no hasty remarks and obedience to the captain. Perseverance; stick to the club and train hard.

Players in the colonies at this time clearly did not set much store by such advice. In 1901, the same newspaper reported:

Rugby seems to be a strangely exciting game in Australia. In a match between Broadford and Seymour every member of the Seymour team was injured, seven seriously. Of the latter, one had a finger broken, another, head battered and one savagely bitten in the face. The sufferings of the umpire when he stopped the game can be imagined. He was not, however, taken home in a bag.

In fact, the very principles of the game were opposed by some. During a visit to Exeter, General Booth, founder of the Salvation Army, expressed the view that a more delightful occupation would be kicking the Devil, not a football!

It was not until 1885 that both a referee and umpires were made mandatory for matches – the duties of the umpires, one appointed by each team, were similar but more extensive than those of the later touch judges. It was originally necessary for a team to appeal for any infringement, as in cricket. Indeed, it was not until 1893 that the RFU agreed to adopt a rule already used in Wales that the referee should blow his whistle as soon as he saw an infringement, rather than waiting for an appeal.

CHAPTER 2
The Pioneer Years

THE LATE 19TH and the early 20th centuries have been called the pioneer years in rugby, with major developments, both locally and nationally. At the national level, the founding of the RFU was followed by separate unions in the other home countries and in the British Empire, and international matches soon followed. In fact, the first international between England and Scotland took place in 1871, almost immediately after the formation of the RFU and before Scotland formed its own union – the Scotland team comprised Scottish members of the RFU, and they won the match. An international against Ireland followed in 1874, and against Wales in 1881.

Locally, the Newton Locomotives, a GWR club, was formed in 1877, bringing the number of rugby-playing teams in Newton to three. Then in 1888 another new club, Newton Rovers, was formed. Some of the names of the early players have reappeared in team lists throughout the history of the club: Dawe, Bearne, Wakeham, Wills, Baker, Elliott, Murrin and Hamlyn.

The first floodlit game in Newton Abbot may have been played as early as 1879. The history of the South Devon Cricket Club, published in 1911 by the *Mid-Devon Advertiser*, recorded: 'In January 1879, Mr Hackworth applied for the use of the cricket ground for a rugby match to be played by the electric light, on the following Friday evening.' There is, however, no record of it having actually taken place.

At the Annual General Meeting of the Newton Volunteers, held at the Newfoundland Inn (since demolished) on 15 April 1886, Lord Clifford, the club President, arrived in full military dress. However, he discovered that, instead of being met by a group of men similarly dressed, most of those present were civilians. He therefore suggested that the club be renamed Newton Football Club, and this was agreed.

The change of name proved to be lucky, as the following season was extremely successful for the club: they won eighteen games, drew two and lost just two, with 48 goals and 37 tries for, and 3 goals and 4 tries against. A large part of their success was down to one remarkable player: a fly half named William Wakeham. Incredible though it may seem, although he was born with just one arm, he was one of Newton's star players. In just one game, against Holborn of Plymouth, he scored ten tries and kicked thirteen goals. Newton won the match by 14 goals and 2 tries to nil, and Wakeham was acclaimed Champion of England. Another star of that season's team was H.B. Tristram, the England full back and a teacher at Newton College.

In the 1892/3 season, Newton extended their range, playing all the main Cornish clubs and beating the Cornish champions, Redruth, home and away. They also played Newport in Newport, a match that attracted 7,000 spectators. They lost narrowly, by 1 goal and 2 tries to 1 goal. They continued this record of success the following season, when they won fifteen of the matches they played to December 1894, losing only to Bristol, 11–3.

At county level, the formation of the Devon Rugby Football Union led to a county trial match at Teignmouth on 14 November 1885, between Exeter and Teignmouth on one side and Plymouth, Paignton, Dartmouth, Newton College and Newton Rifles on the other. The final trial, at Exeter, took place on 5 December, between West and South Devon. E. Paige of Newton captained the South, and four Newton men took part. Paige and F. Williams, also from the Newton club went on to play for Devon against Cornwall at Plymouth on 12 December, a match won by Devon by a goal to a try.

In September 1887 a Devon County Challenge Cup competition was introduced, with fifteen clubs involved: nine from South Devon and six from North Devon. On 3 March 1888, Newton met Tiverton at St Thomas, Exeter, in the first cup final, losing by 1 goal and 2 minors to 4 minors (note the use of the old scoring system, despite the introduction of a new points system by the RFU in 1886). The team was honoured for reaching the final with a dinner at the Bradley Hotel under the chairmanship of the Portreeve of Newton Bushel, Mr Daniel Vile, and presented with caps of black velvet trimmed with silver lace and tassels.

The new, points-based, scoring system seemed to be slow in taking hold. Not only were 'minors' apparently still being used to report on the score in the 1888 cup final, but when Devon played Llanelli in 1889, the score was reported as: Devon 1 dropped goal, 1 save and 2 dead balls, Llanelli 1 try.

The introduction of the cup, and a proposal for a league competition stimulated a great deal of interest in rugby. The 1888 cup final match, for example, attracted a crowd of 10,000, with hundreds of Newton supporters travelling up on special trains. Even less significant games were well attended: Newton's game against Torquay on 12 November 1897 at their new Recreation Ground home, for example, attracted 20,000 spectators. However a certain amount of dissension was caused by the rough play which reportedly resulted from the heightened competitiveness these competitions engendered.

Most of the Devon teams also played charity matches that season in aid of the dependants of the victims of a fire at Exeter Theatre, in which 200 people lost their lives.

On 22 December 1888, Teign Marshes hosted an inter-county game between Devon and Cornwall, with Devon winning by 1 goal to nil. Stork, Gardiner and Ball of Newton all played in the Devon side. On the same day, Newton, unbeaten so far that season and with no points scored against them in ten games, met Crediton, another unbeaten side, winning by 2 goals to 1 try. It is not recorded whether Newton's Devon players were expected to turn out for both matches! The following season, Ball, Bearne and Sellicks of Newton played for Devon. The club continued to provide county players during this decade, and in one game, against Gloucestershire, eleven of the Devon team were from Newton.

The County Championship was inaugurated in 1891, and Devon immediately began to make its mark. They were runners-up in 1895 and again in 1896, and in 1899 became Champions, beating Northumberland 5–0 in Newcastle. The players received 18-carat gold medals at a special banquet at Barnfield Hall, Exeter, and a crowd of 2,000 met the Newton players at the station from a train adorned with a Devon jersey. D.D. Dobson of Newton and Oxford University was take home in a carriage drawn by his supporters and admirers! In 1900 Devon beat Middlesex 15–0 in the semi-final before losing 11–3 to Durham in the final, but in 1901 they gained their revenge by beating Durham 14-3 to win the Championship again. They went on to win the Championship another four times in the next eleven years. Perhaps as a tribute to the county's strength, the 1890s saw what has been described as an 'invasion' of touring sides. In 1898 alone, for example, Devon played host to nine Welsh teams, two from London, one from the Midlands and one from Gloucester.

Newton continued to be a major force in Devon rugby in the 1890s, although the club initially decided not to join the emerging county league. Apart from D.D. Dobson, mentioned above, his brother, W.G. Dobson also played for Devon, as did C.V. Windsor and three others in 1893/4 and W.J. Jackson, who was county full back throughout the 1894/5 season. In addition, H.B.J. Taylor won a Blue at Cambridge (and a second in the 1896/7 season) and E.L.L. Hammond at Oxford. G. Hutchings subsequently played for Oxford University for three successive years, and other notable Newton players of the time included Harry Bartlett, Sims and Frost.

D.D. Dobson

D.D. Dobson went on to play for England against Wales in January 1902, and gained five more England caps. He was also a member of the British team that toured Australia in 1904, where he became embroiled in a fracas in the game against Northern Districts. He was alleged to have disagreed with a decision of the referee, and was sent off. The British captain, D.R. Bodwell-Sivright, thereupon withdrew his team from the field, saying that Dobson had not made the offending remark, and was one of the quietest and most gentlemanly players in the team, and the referee's decision was an insult to him and to the team. Despite his international fame, Dobson was dedicated to Newton. He said he had learned the game watching the club play and playing for them as a young man, and he had no desire to play elsewhere.

In the 1894/5 season Newton ran a second team for the first time, and there were no less than nineteen teams in the town: two from the Newton Abbot club itself, three from Newton College, two from Newton Locomotives, two church teams and a team each from Newton Rovers, Newton Hornets, Newton Blues, Aller Vale, Newton Grammar School, Newton Association, Wolborough Hill School, Bradley Rangers, Highweek Rushers and Sun Court Flashers! Bovey Tracey also had a good team. Newton Rovers, and another team, Newton Juniors, were incorporated into the Newton club in 1896. Many of the teams had nicknames: Exeter were known as the Ever Faithful, and Torquay as the Ladies' Pets. There is no record of a nickname for Newton in the early years, but in the early years of the twentieth century they were apparently known as Harry Bartlett and Co., a reference to one of the team's major players, who became captain.

In 1889, a wooden grandstand with a capacity of 150 was erected at Teign Marshes, at a cost of £25. However, the club's days at their birthplace were numbered. At the AGM on 26 August 1896, there was a heated discussion about a proposed move to the new Recreation Ground, created with 5,000 cartloads of earth (at a cost of 1d per load), in the centre of town. The directors of the company set up to run the Recreation Ground offered to let the club use it every Saturday, four Thursdays per season, on Good Friday and on Boxing Day, for which the club eventually offered a fee of £30 per season. However, the Committee were not disposed to leave Teign Marches, and it was not until 1897 that they finally agreed the terms of their occupation. A promenade concert, cycle parade and al fresco ball were held to raise funds. The move was good for attendance: the new season saw a doubling of the attendance figures, and as we have seen, one game between Newton and Torquay attracted a crowd of over 2,000.

The change of ground saw a change in the club's colours, from the regimental red and green to red and yellow. This alteration did not last long, however. Universally condemned as 'vile', they were very soon changed again to red, black and amber. Then in 1903 the present 'all white' strip was adopted.

The early years of the twentieth century saw the emergence of a man who was to become one of the great names in the history of the club: Percy Hodge. He made his debut for the First XV in February 1904 against Exeter, a game that was drawn 6–6. He played again the following season, Harry Bartlett's first as captain, which started off disastrously, with a 48–0 whitewash by Plymouth, followed immediately by a 9–0 defeat to Bristol. Despite that start, supporters of the club awarded merit caps to the team, including Percy Hodge, Harry Bartlett, H. Harvey, W. Neck, H. Field, S. Mogridge, H. Baker, J. Dove, J. Winsbarrow, R. Sharp, F. Heath, W. Harris, F. Tozer and E. Mallett.

CHAPTER 3
Overseas Visitors

The Globe Hotel, 1906

THE 1905/6 SEASON was a momentous one for the club, and for Newton rugby fans, as New Zealand, on their first tour of Britain, made their headquarters in the town. Arriving at Plymouth in the early hours of a bright September day, they travelled to Newton Abbot by train. They stayed at the Globe Hotel ('more an old rambling country house than a hotel'), and trained with the Newton team at the Recreation Ground. The townspeople took them to their hearts and laid on smoking concerts and other entertainments.

Not much was expected of them in terms of rugby, however. They were, after all, 'colonials', and the newspapers patronisingly reported that, although they were superbly fit, they had really come here to learn the finer points of the game. And who better to teach them than Devon, former County Champions (who were about to become County Champions again)? It was something of a shock, therefore, when the visitors beat the county 55–4 at Exeter in their first game. Such was the sense of disbelief, that some newspapers reported a 55–4 victory to Devon! When they returned to Newton Abbot at midnight, however, they were greeted like native sons: several hundred people turned out to greet them, the Town Band was on hand, and two charabancs took them in state to their hotel, where the manager welcomed them with a speech of congratulations.

Following that victory, the All Blacks as they were becoming known, went on a tour of Great Britain, playing a number of county and club teams and beating them all by a wide margin (41–0 against Cornwall, for example, and 63–0 against Hartlepool). On their return to Newton Abbot on 31 October, they were again given a tremendous welcome. In the words of their manager, George Dixon, it was 'like coming back home'. And the captain, Dave Gallagher later wrote: 'Until we go over to the great unknown, the welcome given to us will never be effaced from the memories of any of us.' Each member of the team was given an inscribed mug from the Royal Aller Vale Pottery, presented by Hexter, Humpherson & Co.

Then in November and December they were off again, convincingly beating England, Scotland and Ireland. They lost to Wales 3–0, however, following a controversially disallowed try by the All Black wing, Deans. It seemed that the 'mother country' could learn a thing or two from its colonial offspring! They left England for France on New Year's Eve, and continued their tour with victories against France and two Canadian sides.

After the departure of the All Blacks, Devon became County Champions again by defeating their old rivals Durham 16–3. At a local level, the Newton team was developing, with names that were to become part of the club's history, names such as Bartlett, Sharpe, Squires, and of course Percy Hodge, who in 1906 became captain of the local cricket team in addition to his captaincy of the rugby club.

Newton Abbot played host to another colonial team in 1906. The South Africans were also on their first tour, and like the All Blacks, impressed their British opponents with the standard of their play. It was on this tour that they acquired the nickname the Springboks, by which they are still known. They only stayed in Newton Abbot for a week in October, while they prepared for their meeting with the new County Champions in Devonport on the 17th – a match they won 22–6. Perhaps because of the shortness of their visit, however, they were not as popular in the town as the New Zealanders. As one account says: 'They did not create the favourable impression left by the All Blacks and were referred to as a quiet, withdrawn lot.' The team went on to beat Wales and Ireland, lose to Scotland and draw with England.

Yet another group of colonials visited Newton Abbot in 1908 – this time the Australian team, also on their first tour. They arrived in September and made their headquarters in the town for their stay in Devon because, they said, they had heard from their New Zealand cousins how welcoming the people were. They were welcomed at the railway station by Mr A.J. Murrin, Chairman of the Urban District Council, and Mr C.L. Vicary, Chairman of the Newton Abbot Rugby Club. They, in their turn, gave three cheers for the club.

On their arrival in Plymouth, the tourists were asked by a local reporter to choose a nickname, as several were being used at the time. In a vote among team members they chose 'Wallabies', a name by which they have been known ever since. They spent every morning training at the Recreation Ground, and the afternoons visiting Dartmoor and other popular tourist areas. They caused a great deal of interest in the town, as they walked about in their light blue sweaters and jackets, dark blue shorts and straw hats. Their emblem was the waratal, an indigenous Australian flower. Another point of interest was the mascot one of the team had brought with him – a carpet snake which died while they were here.

As was the case with their All Black and Springbok predecessors, Australia were not rated very highly by the local press, but this time perhaps with more reason: out of the twelve internationals they had played before this tour, they had won only one. However, they managed to beat Devon 24–3 at Devonport, despite playing with only fourteen men after forward Peter Burge broke his leg. They then went on a tour of England and Wales, losing to Wales but beating England. They also played in the London Olympics in October, one of only two teams to enter! Ireland and Scotland turned down the chance to compete, and France withdrew at the last minute. So Australia played Cornwall, the County Champions representing England, in the only match, and beat them 8–3 to win the gold medal.

New Zealand Rugby Football Team, 1905-6	
Harold L. Abbot	W. Mackrell
Ernest E. Booth	Alex McDonald
S. Casey	D. McGregor
J. T. Corbett	H. J. Mynott
W. Cunningham	F. Newton
R. G. Deans	G. W. Nicholson
Jas. Duncan	Fred Roberts
Geo. Gillett	C. E. Seeling
L. Glasgow	G. W. Smith
W. S. Glenn	J. C. Sullivan
Eric T. Harper	H. D. Thompson
Jas. Hunter	Geo. A. Tyler
W. Johnston	W. J. Wallace
Captain: D. Gallaher	
Vice-Captain: J. W. Stead	
Manager: G. H. Dixon	

CHAPTER 4

The Second Golden Age

IF THE 1890s was regarded a golden age in the history of the club, the years leading up to the First World War were another. The 1906/7 season started superbly, with wins over Exeter 42–3, Redruth 18–3, Exmouth 6–0, Sidmouth 26–8, Paignton 6–0, the RNE College 11–9, Taunton 18–3, Torquay 13–3, Stroud 22–0 and Welsh team Danygraig 6–0. It carried on in similar vein, and they were unbeaten until March, and ended the season having lost only five of their thirty-five games.

The 1908/9 season was marred by a lawsuit that made rugby history. During a match at Paignton, the referee, J.R. Frost, sent off one of the Newton forwards, Lethbridge. As Frost left the field, he was struck violently on the side of the head, allegedly by Lethbridge. The Devon Union refused to deal with the case, and proceedings for assault were initiated in the police court. Lethbridge was found guilty and sentenced to a month in prison. Lethbridge's solicitor, Mr Hutchings, appealed and a public subscription was opened to meet the costs of the case. The appeal was heard at the Devon Quarter Sessions on 5 January, and created a great deal of public interest, with local newspapers running special supplements with verbatim reports. The appeal was allowed with costs, and Lethbridge was met on his return by thousands of well-wishers, plus the town band.

Despite the furore created by this case, the club had another excellent season in 1908/9, being unbeaten at home, and scoring more than 500 points in a season for the first time in their history. They beat Exeter 9–0 in the Devon Senior Cup, but then lost to the powerful Devonport Albion in the final by a try to nil. The star of the season was Percy Hodge, although Bunclark was brilliant at full back.

Newton's sister team, Kingsteignton, won the Devon Junior Cup in both 1910 and 1911, and Newton achieved another clean sweep of home matches in 19010/11. The club again won the Torquay division of the Devon Senior Cup, beating Torquay 5–4, and then the mighty Devonport Albion 16–5 at home. Unfortunately, they then suffered a surprise defeat in the final to a lesser-known Plymouth side. Their unbeaten home record continued in 1911/12, and they finished the season with only three losses out of thirty-seven games. They conceded just 134 points in the season, and scored 610 – a remarkable total at that time, and one that was not exceeded for many years. The season was marred by a feud with Devonport Albion, however. Newton having won the Torquay Division of the Devon Cup, the two clubs were drawn against each other in the semi-final of the Devon Junior Cup, to be played in Plymouth on 9 March. In their official programme, Devonport made various insinuations and allegations against Newton, including one of 'ancient brutality'. Newton demanded that these statements be publicly withdrawn, and when Devonport demurred, they refused to play them. The Torquay Division runners-up, Torquay, were invited to play in the semi-final instead, and Newton played Redruth. The top scorer that season was wing three quarter Len Murrin, but Percy Hodge again excelled himself as captain. He also scored a total of 1,198 runs for the Devon cricket team in the 1911 season.

The 1912/13 season did not start well: Newton lost their unbeaten home record in September, when they lost to Devonport Services 15–8. The rest of the season was marred by the controversy over attempts to introduce the Northern Union code in Devon (see Chapter 5). The following season started well, with the club remaining unbeaten until December. Things went downhill rapidly after that, however: they went on to lose ten matches before April!

End-of-season celebrations had always taken the form of dinners and smoking concerts (live music concerts attended by men only), but at this time the advent of charabancs allowed the players and their supporters to travel further. They therefore took to going out to Dartmoor, where they had a picnic (with enough liquid refreshment to supply an Army corps!), followed by cricket matches.

Devon were also having something of a golden era during this period, and on 25 February 1911 beat Yorkshire in Leeds to become County Champions for the fifth time. They were helped in no small measure by the men of Newton Abbot: in 1909/10 Newton provided six players to the Devon county side (and one to Cornwall). The Devon players were three-quarters Paddon and Prudence, half backs Squires and Hodge, and forwards Mason and Tozer. Barrett played for Cornwall. The Newton schoolboy Cecil Davey, played scrum half for England against Wales. Newton also beat Welsh side Pontypool at Pontypool, reputedly the first English side to do so. In the 1912/13 season six Newton players were in the Devon team: Hodge, Donaldson, Benthall, Mills, Sharp and Hacker (who, according to reports, was well named!). Hodge also performed brilliantly for Devon in 1914, earning the nickname 'the All Whites wizard'. He was also considered for an England trial, before the war intervened.

CHAPTER 5

The 'Great Rugby Rumpus'

THE DEVON RUGBY world in general, and Newton Abbot's club in particular, were torn apart during 1912 and 1913 by what the press dubbed the 'great rugby rumpus'. It had actually started twenty years earlier in northern England, but in the three years leading up to the First World War, it reached the West Country.

In 1892, two Yorkshire clubs had been charged with professionalism by the RFU because they gave their players 'broken time' payments – compensation for wages lost when they were playing for their clubs. Yorkshire in their turn complained that the RFU's decision-making was dominated by southern clubs, even though there were more clubs in the north, mainly because it was more difficult for northern representatives to travel to London for meetings. A proposal to allow 'broken time' payments was defeated at the RFU in 1893, and in 1895, with the support of a number of Lancashire clubs, the Yorkshiremen formed the Northern Rugby Football Union (usually known as the Northern Union), and the clubs involved resigned from the RFU. The RFU took such a hard line against the new body that even purely amateur sides were banned if they played against Northern Union teams. This led to most amateur northern clubs leaving the RFU and joining the Northern Union, and by 1904, this organisation had more members than the RFU. The clubs initially played by RFU rules, but over the early years, they began to diverge until the two forms became quite distinct. In the 1920s the Northern Union changed its name to the Northern Rugby Football League, and the terms 'rugby union' and 'rugby league' began to be used.

The Northern Union was keen to spread its version of the game further afield, and it was enthusiastically adopted in Australia and New Zealand. In the UK, however, they met with less success. After several failed attempts to establish a foothold in Wales, the NU turned its attention to the West Country. In the summer of 1912 they made a bid to establish a Western League, and initially nine clubs expressed an interest – Redruth, Falmouth and Camborne in Cornwall, Exeter, Exmouth, Torquay, Newton Abbot and Plymouth in Devon, and Bridgwater in Somerset. Several others adopted a 'wait and see' position.

On 24 August, the Newton Abbot committee resolved that, since twelve clubs were needed for a viable league, they would not pursue the matter that season – a decision that a Northern Union representative called a death blow to any hopes of establishing the northern code in the area. Torquay came to a similar decision. Recriminations followed against those who had tried to break away; the Newton Treasurer, W.A. Bond, who was also a member of the Devon RFU committee, plus two other Newton officials, were asked to explain their actions, and were subsequently suspended, along with two officials from Torquay, one from Plymouth and one from Teignmouth. Ten players were also suspended, including E. Mallett of Newton Abbot. On 19 October the RFU held a full inquiry at Exeter, as a result of which Bond and Mallett were expelled and two other officials, F. Valley and H. Phillips, suspended until 14 April, along with Percy Hodge, the captain. There were other expulsions and suspensions across Devon, including the majority of Devonport Albion players.

This was by no means the end of the matter, however. The expulsions and suspensions caused uproar and, in a mood of rebellion, a public meeting was held in the Town Hall, Newton Abbot, presided over by W.A. Bond, the expelled Devon committee member. He was supported by expelled committee members from other clubs, and by his colleague H. Phillips. In view of the fact that eight Devon and Cornwall clubs had initially favoured switching, the meeting passed a resolution calling for the adoption of Northern Union rules, with only three votes against. Mr C.L. Vicary, the Newton Abbot Chairman stated that the remainder of his committee stood firm for the RFU.

In January 1913, the Northern Union secured the Paignton RFC ground, with all its equipment., and a Northern Union committee was formed in Torquay, including H. Phillips and W.A Bond of Newton Abbot. At the same time NU clubs were formed in Torquay and Plymouth. The first match under NU rules was played at Paignton on 18 January between these two clubs, with an admission charge of 3d (1s 3d in the stand), attracting 2,000 spectators. The same day, a depleted Torquay RFU side was defeated in Newton Abbot. The South Devon Northern Union camp received a boost when, at a special meeting, the Teignmouth committee and players voted unanimously to go over to the new code, and practically all the players signed on. They lost their first two games, 20–5 to Torquay and 9–3 to Plymouth.

The number of Devon clubs playing by Northern Union rules increased to four on 15 March, when it was announced that a committee had been formed in Newton Abbot to establish an NU club – this on the very day that the Devon committee was meeting, also in Newton Abbot, to discuss their strategy for combating the northern incursion! The Newton committee comprised two of the original rebels, H. Phillips as Chairman, and W.A. Bond as Secretary, with S.P. Wyatt as Treasurer, and a committee of W. Boney, E. Willcocks, A.T. Thomas, S. Badcock and W. Crossman. A combination Northern Union team toured Devon at Easter that year to play the four NU sides. The match against Newton Abbot took place at the Recreation Ground on Good Friday in front of a record crowd, with the tourists recording a narrow win.

This was the first and last NU or rugby league game to be played in Newton Abbot. The Northern Union decided that it would not be worth continuing their attempts to get a Western League off the ground the following season, and the four Devon NU teams quietly faded away. Teignmouth effectively had no club in the 1913/14 season, since virtually the whole of their team had signed up to the NU code the previous year. They did not re-establish themselves as an RFU club until after the First World War.

CHAPTER 6
The Third Golden Age

THE OUTBREAK OF WAR brought an almost complete halt to rugby in Devon. The Newton President, D.B. Webster, gave a suitably downbeat assessment at the Annual General Meeting of the club in July: 'Even if it lasts two or three months only, the loss of income will be considerable.' On 29 August, at a conference of Devon senior clubs at Newton Abbot, the Devon President, G.H. Smith, suggested that games should go on as near normally as possible. However, Mr C.L. Vicary of Newton Abbot said that if the war went on for many weeks, those connected with his club 'would be too busy elsewhere'. As it happened, of course, the war went on for considerably more than a few weeks, and although the meeting decided that each club should make its own arrangements, very little rugby was played in the county between 1914 and 1918, apart from occasional charity matches.

It was not long after the ending of hostilities, however, before things returned to normal in Devon rugby – or at least as close to normal as the circumstances allowed, given that many of the pre-war players had been killed or wounded during the conflict. The 'All Whites wizard' Percy Hodge was among the latter, having lost a leg. He carried on his association with Newton and Devon rugby, however: he coached the Newton team and became President of the DRFU in 1950 and 1951. In February 1919, the Devon clubs agreed to resume normal fixtures as soon as possible, and a Devon team played against teams from the New Zealand and Australian services. They beat New Zealand Services 3–0, but lost to the Australians 6–3. Tommy Emmett of Newton was the outstanding player of the team, which also included his club-mates H. Bunclark and F. Tozer. 'Normal service' included the resumption of the Devon Senior and Junior Cups later in the year.

With regard to the 'great rumpus', the post-war mood was one of reconciliation: there was a general amnesty for those who had crossed over to the new code, and rugby union started again as if the whole flirtation with the Northern Union had never happened – or almost. In fact, several Newton Abbot players went north to play in the Northern League: 'Ginger' Wood, George Prudence and Paddon, later joined by Short.

The first full season following the war saw the beginning of Newton Abbot's third golden age. Bunclark and Emmett played again for Devon, and were joined by Bob Sharp. Sharp also played for the South against England in the first international trial, and again for the Rest against England in the final trial. Although he was praised in the local press, however, he was not selected for the England team. Later in the

Newton Abbot 'Old Boys' 1920/21

season, he, Short and Emmett played for Devon. Rowse was later also picked for the county.

The club was unbeaten at home that season, and over the next seven years lost only 50 out of 274 games, accumulating a total of 2,865 points in the process. And the matches were increasingly popular. Despite an increase in the admission charge to 8d (1s for the enclosure and 1s 6d for the stand), the club attracted about 20,000 spectators over the 1919/20 season; Torquay alone brought 2,000 supporters for their 'derby' match against Newton on 19 February. Among the club's scalps that season were Plymouth, Torquay and Taunton (all defeated twice), the Royal Navy, the United Services and Welsh side Pontypridd.

The 1st XV went on tour to Wales, losing narrowly to Ebbw Vale and Pontypool. They thoroughly enjoyed their visit to Ebbw Vale, but Pontypool was a different matter. There was a certain amount of history between the clubs, Newton having been the first English club to beat Pontypool, back in 1910. Three Newton players had to be carried off the field.

On 12 February 1921, Newton beat Torquay 6–3 at the Recreation Ground in the Devon Senior Cup, in front of a crowd estimated at 8,000. Two matches against Paignton were drawn, even after extra time, but Newton eventually triumphed 4–3. The team played Plymouth Albion in the final, again before 8,000 spectators, but lost 11–3, after losing Tommy Emmett in the opening minutes. The 1920/21 season saw seven Newton players playing for Devon: A. Hugo, L. Taylor, W. Hambly, C. Mole, G. Rowse, E. Warren, and G. Gempton. The same seven represented the county the following season.

Unfortunately, Gempton blotted his copybook the following season; he was sent off during a match against Plymouth Albion on 31 December, although the team still managed a 6–5 victory. Albion refused to play Newton for the next two seasons. In the same match, the referee, Mr J. Rowe, claimed that an unknown player called him a cheat, and he ended the game six minutes before time. There were victories against two Cornish clubs, Hayle 9–0 and Redruth 14–5, and against Welsh club Penarth 19–3.

The 1922/3 and 1923/4 seasons were probably the most successful ever for Newton Abbot teams. They opened 1922/3 by beating Barnstaple 42–8. In the Devon Senior Cup semi-final, they beat Exmouth 6–3, and in the final beat local rivals Torquay 7–0 at home. Phillips scored a drop goal and Captain Rowse a try. They were apparently presented with parcels of sausages and bacon – although at the annual dinner they also received gold medals! In 1923/24 they started by beating Bath 11–0 and were unbeaten until Christmas. They claimed the best record of any senior club in the country, losing only four of their forty-one games, and beat Torquay in the Devon Senior Cup final for the second year in succession. In fact, they beat Torquay four times; their other scalps included Redruth (twice), United Services and Bridgwater.

They were deprived of a Devon Senior Cup hat trick by Exmouth, who beat them in the 1924/5 final 10–0. Press reports commented on the spirit in which the game was played. One said:

[It] will long provide a pleasant memory for the five or six thousand spectators who witnessed the match. The teams demonstrated that in a desperately hard-fought game it is possible to have good football, and that interest in a cup-tie need not necessarily hang merely upon the issue.

After the match, the Newton Secretary, Mr R.S. Stephens, wrote to his Exmouth counterpart:

I have been requested by the Committee and players of the Newton Club to convey to you their congratulations on your Club's winning of the Devon Senior Cup this season. Having tasted the sweets of victory before, we can now accept the sours of defeat. We wish your Club every success.

A similar sense of solidarity was displayed by Newton, when they gave all the gate money at a match with Plymouth Albion the same season to the latter club, who were in financial difficulties.

Unfortunately, not all Senior Cup games were played in a similar spirit. The cup engendered such high feeling that many games were stopped before full time, and clubs were refusing to play against each other and cancelling fixtures with alarming regularity. Indeed, in the 1925/6 season, Newton itself withdrew from the competition. They returned in style in 1926/7, however, winning the competition yet again by beating their old rivals Exmouth 17–0 at Exeter. It was, by all accounts, another good, open game, but with some unfortunate injuries – the Exmouth captain, Sansom, was carried off with a broken leg, while W. Hambly, one of three brothers in the Newton team, had to leave the field with a broken collar bone. The other two Hamblys made their mark, however: C. Hambly scored a try, which F. Hambly converted. On their return to Newton Abbot, they were met by thousands of supporters, the Town Band and the Chairman of the Urban District Council, Mr John Dolbear, who gave them a civic welcome, with speeches and the singing of the National Anthem at the Clock Tower.

The club had a good 1926/7 season generally, although not as successful as in previous years. The tally was: played 44, won 26, drawn 7, lost 11, points for 506, points against 262.

The Reserves were also going through a purple patch. They won the 1920/1 Devon Junior Cup by beating Exmouth Reserves 12–3 in the final in Torquay. A huge crowd turned out to welcome them back, including of course the Town Band, and the team were presented with medals. Their record for the season was: won 28, lost 3, points for 505, points against 84. They lost narrowly to the same side the following season, 6–5. In 1924/5, however, they were victorious again. They were coached by Alfie Johns, who was to be a trainer for the All Whites for the next forty years. Newton Juniors won the Intermediate Cup in its first season (1922/3) by beating Keppel Albion of Plymouth 17–3, and won it again the following year. They continued to do well: in 1926/7, for example, they lost only one game.

The 1920/1 season also saw an innovation at the club. Mr W. Reeve decided to explore the possibility of establishing a formal group of supporters for the club. The club Chairman, Mr B.D. Webster, supported the idea, as did Percy Hodge, and on 9 November 1920 the inaugural meeting of the Newton Supporters Club was held at the Recreation Ground. Seventy members were enrolled there and then, and within a week the number had increased to 120, including one lady. By the end of the season, the membership stood at 171, each paying a subscription of 2s. It continued to go from strength to strength, and in 1927 it was invited to second two members onto the club committee. In the same year, its President, Major V.L. Burnett, coined its motto, 'Deeds not words'.

In 1923, Mr C.L. Vicary, a local mill owner who had been President of the Newton club for many years (and continued in that role right up to the outbreak of the Second World War), was elected President of the Devon RFU; he continued to serve the county until 1938.

The club said a sad but grateful farewell to George Rowse in 1927. After a playing career spanning twenty years, including seven as Captain of the All Whites (which he described as the most enjoyable), he had decided to call it a day. He had made a significant contribution to the team, and had led them to three Devon Senior Cup victories. Soon afterwards, he moved to Paignton.

Newton Abbots 'sister club', Kingsteington, 1923

CHAPTER 7
The Pre-War Years

THE DECADES LEADING up to the Second World War were a time of mixed fortunes for Newton Abbot rugby. The club resumed fixtures against Torquay in 1927/8 after a lapse of a few years, but overall they had a mixed season. There was a fall-off in gate receipts, as some spectators deserted rugby to follow the newly established professional soccer team in Torquay. One highlight for the town, though not directly for the club, was the selection of Reg Lodge of Wolborough Hill School for the English Schools team to play Wales in 1928.

There was something akin to the passing of the old guard in 1928 and 1929. In 1928 the club mourned the loss of Francis Valley, who had long been a great stalwart of the club. At the Annual General Meeting in July 1929, Bob Stephens's 21-year reign as Secretary came to an end, when he was defeated in the election by T. French. As it happened, neither survived to see in the new season: Mr Stephens died eight months after the AGM and Mr French a few days later.

The depression in South Wales brought many of that area's top players to Devon, looking for employment, and one of the first qualifications some employers asked for was an ability to play first-class rugby. Torquay developed a superb team in the late 1920s and early 1930s, with Welsh internationals Delahay, Richards, Twose and Scourfield joining them. In the 1930/1 season, for example, they were unbeaten until January, when they lost 13–3 to Newport, having previously beaten Cardiff 156–11. Despite this, however, it was Paignton who won the Devon Senior Cup in 1931, and Brixham in 1932. Despite the arrival in Newton Abbot of another Welshman, F. Webb from Crosskeys, the club did not have a good couple of seasons. Flooding and consistent bad weather caused the cancellation of many fixtures in both the 1928/9 and 1929/30 seasons, affecting the club's finances. Moreover, a succession of injuries did not help the club's fortunes.

On a more positive note, in 1928 'Dacco' Veale and Eddie Elliott were selected for Devon. In the same year Tommy Bowen made his first appearance for the club, and went on to play for Devon and make a name for himself as a full back. In 1931 he was acclaimed as a hero of Devon's game against British Police at Newton Abbot, which the county won 9–4. He was later followed by his three sons, and the whole family gave great service to the club. In 1930, the club started wearing letters on their jerseys to distinguish the various positions, starting with 'A' for the full back.

The club had much better seasons in 1931/2 and 1932/3, beating a greatly improving Plymouth Albion side 8–6 in 1931, and cementing their success with wins over the

Midland team Moseley and West Country rivals Bath. In 1933 they managed a draw against Albion – no mean feat, considering that Albion beat mighty Cardiff home and away. 'Nugget' Northcott and 'Spike' Elliott were selected for Devon, and the team's drop-goal specialist, Harold Evans, back from foreign service and playing behind what he described as a 'magnificent West County pack', helped the team to notable success in that season. They beat Exeter 20–3 in 1932, and went on to achieve an unbeaten run of sixteen matches until beaten by Redruth 12–3 on 11 February 1933. They ended the season with only six defeats out of thirty-eight games. In fact, despite Plymouth Albion's growing success, it was Newton Abbot and Torquay who were generally considered the best two teams in Devon by 1935. So when they met on 2 February of that year, there was great excitement; it was a very close-fought game, which Torquay won 8–7. In the same season, Newton paid their first ever visit to Penzance, and won 11–8. They finished that season by beating Old Haberdashers of London 35–6 and Moseley 3–0.

Apart from the excitement of the All Blacks' visit (see Chapter 8), the 1935/6 season was something of a disaster for the All Whites. The Recreation Ground, now in private hands, was unavailable for the whole season, owing to the installation of a new drainage system and returfing of the pitch. There was even talk of suspending the club for a season. A statement by the committee said:

> Your Committee have learned with alarm and regret that the Recreation Ground is not available for the coming season, and in view of this and lack of suitable alternative accommodation, recommend suspension of playing operations for the coming season and until the ground is again fit for play.

Eventually, however, they compromised by playing at Osborne Park, a public open space not much bigger than a rugby pitch and almost entirely surrounded by buildings. The first match there was against Teignmouth, which Newton won by a single try, scored by Sid Rowe, one of the character of the club, who played for Newton for several seasons, and went on to become a referee, and a trainer of the Devon team for many years.

Although all rugby was cancelled on the death of King George V on 25 January 1936, many more of Newton's games were cancelled because of the state of their makeshift ground. Several players became disenchanted and moved to other clubs – three to Torquay alone. Because it was impossible to charge an admission fee, the club's finances suffered significantly. In a sporting gesture, both Teignmouth and Plymouth Albion donated home gates to Newton, in Plymouth's case repaying a favour Newton had granted them some years before when they themselves were in financial difficulty. Overall, it was a season to forget. The club's record reads: played 26, won 11, lost 14, points for 169, points against 303.

Things did begin to look up with the return to the Recreation Ground the following season, and the appearance of a bright new star in the form of 'Shoppy' Sanders, a convert from football, who kicked three conversions in his first game, reached 100 points by February and finished the season with a record 138. The following season his tally was 133, and he played for Devon. Newton beat the touring Welsh Academicals 10–8 on Christmas Day 1936. The 1937/8 season saw the emergence of several impressive new players, including fly half Arthur Kift, who with Mickey Sims formed a famously successful half-back partnership. He starred in a 5–0 victory over Exeter, followed by a 6–3 win over Plymouth Albion. The other Newton 'immortal' to emerge in 1937 was Gordon 'Doc' Emmett. Both he and Kift went on to play for Devon and Newton Abbot well into the 1950s. Other new players who came to dominate the team were C. Luscombe and P. Howard.

Their arrival helped to boost the club's performance, and they had a very good 1938/9 season; 'Shoppy' Saunders continued his successful run, with 111 points in the season. They were therefore looking forward to an even more successful 1939/40, but Hitler had other ideas. Training ceased almost as soon as it had begun, and on 3 September the country was at war. Scratch games were arranged, including with a wartime team called Torquay Albion, as well as Paignton, Exeter, Plymouth and Army and Navy teams. However, in March 1940, the Chairman, Percy Hodge, announced that the club would no longer play, as it was becoming increasingly difficult to raise a team. Having only just cleared their debts, the club's financial situation no doubt also influenced the decision.

Newton Juniors also came into their own during this period; in 1928/9, for example, under the guidance of Ern Flood, they won sixteen matches, drew two and lost only one, and in 1932, Graham Hollow and Bill Towell were chosen for an English Schools trial. In the 1933/4 season, they lost only four games, their captain, B. Horrell, scoring eighty points.

Newton Supporters' Club continued to thrive, under the chairmanship of Mr T. Tarr, and raised very welcome funds for the club through the sale of programmes, cushions and advertisements, as well as social events. A ladies' committee was also formed, on which Mrs B. Bartlett played a prominent part. Their success was in sharp contrast to the situation in Teignmouth, where the rugby club refused to recognise their supporters' club and requested it to disband. The Supporters' Club's fund-raising efforts were in greater and greater demand, as the effects of the advent of professional football continued to be felt. In August 1934, a public appeal had to be made for funds, as it did again in 1935, when the team was forced to play in Osborne Park. In 1938 it was again necessary to ask for contributions. Torquay offered to play two extra games at Newton to boost gate receipts, and the Juniors also contributed. Then, during the summer of 1939 the *Mid Devon Advertiser* launched an appeal for a further £100, which drew a very good response, with contributions coming in from South Devon Cricket Club, Sidmouth and Torquay rugby clubs, the Newton Abbot Bowling Club, former captain George Rowe, Major Mills from India and many town sportsmen.

Newton Juniors
1928/9

Devon 1902

Rest of England 1902

Newton Abbot 1904-05

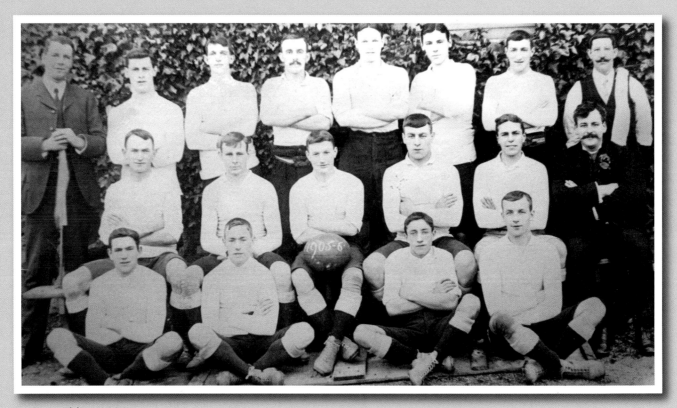

Newton Abbot 1906

1906-07

1907/08

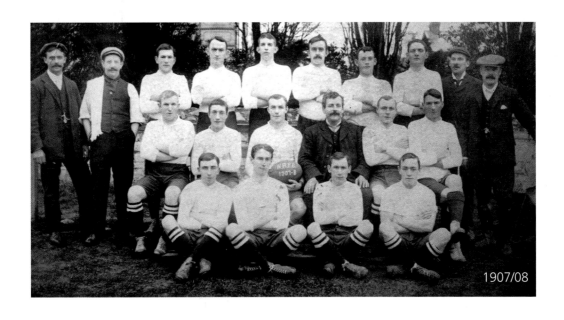

1907/08

1910-11

1920

1920-21

1920-21

1922

1924

NEWTON ABBOT
RUGBY CLUB
RESERVES
DEVON JUNIOR CUP
WINNERS
1924 1925

Aerial view over Newton Abbot, 1928

1930

1930-31

1931-32

1932-33

1934-35

1935-36

1936-37

CHAPTER 8

The Return of the All Blacks

ON 20 AUGUST 1924, the All Blacks returned to Newton Abbot to a tumultuous welcome. They were led in procession to their headquarters at the Globe Hotel, with people lining the route and hanging out of windows, waving and cheering. There was a programme of entertainments over the next twelve days, as well as matches against Devon and Cornwall, before they went up-country to continue their tour. It was all reminiscent of the previous visit in 1905; indeed, the All Black Captain, Cliff Porter, said in his speech, 'The 1905 players always speak in high terms of Newton Abbot, and they have asked us to convey to you their best wishes.' And one team member sent a cable home, saying, 'Home coming of All Blacks was one of the greatest demonstrations of welcome ever witnessed in the town.'

The team beat a Devon side that included Newtonians A. Hugo and W. Mole 11–0 and Cornwall 29–0, before going on to win every game they played, including victories against Ireland 6–0, Wales 19–0 and England 17–11. Scotland refused to play them because of a dispute over expenses. In their twenty-eight games, they scored 654 points and conceded only 98, a record that earned them the nickname 'The Invincibles'.

They were followed in 1926 by a Maori team, which played Devon, losing 20–0 but do not appear to have visited Newton Abbot.

Eight years later, the Newton Abbot Urban District Council, on hearing that another All Black tour was planned for 1935/6, wrote to the New Zealand authorities, inviting them to make the town their base again, an invitation that was gladly accepted. Preparations were made to welcome them in style, and Mr H.T. Luke undertook the editing of a special souvenir booklet. On arrival at the railway station, the team was greeted by Mr J.L.B. Elms, President of the Supporters' Club, and a huge crowd, who had been waiting for an hour in the rain. They were then taken in procession to the Globe Hotel. Here they received a civic reception, and at the insistence of the crowd made a 'royal' appearance on the balcony. The event warranted a full front-page report in the *Mid Devon Advertiser*. The Chairman of the Council, Mr L. Coomb welcomed the visitors with the following words:

We Newtonians have placed all the town's amenities at your disposal and therefore you are, as it were, freemen of Newton Abbot. I congratulate you on picking out the best district of the most glorious county in England for your

The All Blacks
team which
toured the UK in
1905/6

*training. I wish you on behalf of the town every success in your tour, and hope
you will be particularly free from accidents.*

In response, the All Blacks' Manager, Mr V.R. Meredith, presented the council with a
magnificent Maori jewel casket and a chairman's gavel made of green stone, and said:

*I may tell you that we, in New Zealand, were all familiar with Devon in our
schoolboy studies. We have read about the great doings of the men in Devon in
the past and the great part they have played in history ....We also know of the
beauties of this county, which is known throughout the whole Empire as glorious
Devon.*

*We have heard from the members of the teams ....who visited here in 1905 and
1924, of the wonderful hospitality showered on them on those visits......everyone
of them carried away the most vivid recollections of the kindness shown to them
at Newton Abbot, and they have never forgotten it. They wish me ... to let you
know how they feel about it ... When it was known that you were willing to
have us and that we were able to commence our training for our long and
arduous tour in this town of Newton Abbot, which we know to be a great
sporting centre of Devon, we were only to glad to avail ourselves of the
opportunity of accepting your hospitality. We know that with the beautiful
Devon air and the hospitality we shall leave here thoroughly fortified for the
long and arduous tour ahead of us. I wish to thank you again for the great
welcome you have given to us on our arrival.*

The hospitality provided by the town over the ten days of their stay included visits to
Dartmoor, the zoo and the races, a gymkhana, a ball, speedboat rides, games of golf,
tours of historical places and honorary membership of all local sports clubs. The one
fly in the ointment was the state of the Recreation Ground (see Chapter 7), only a
small part of which could be used for training. Full training therefore had to be
transferred to Paignton. The team played a combined Devon and Cornwall side on
14 September 1935 in Plymouth, winning 35–6, before touring the rest of the British
Isles. They were not as successful as their predecessors, losing their internationals
against Wales 13–12 and England 13–0, although they beat Scotland 18–8 and Ireland
17–9. Even against club and regional sides they did not have a clean sweep; they lost
to Swansea and drew with Ulster.

The All Blacks
an enduring legacy

FROM THEIR FIRST visit in 1905/6, through to subsequent tours in the 1920s and 30s, the presence of the New Zealand tourists has provided a lasting legacy for rugby enthusiasts in Devon, with Newton Abbot central to each visit. On each occasion the tourists enjoyed celebrity status in the town, none more so than in the tour of 1935/6 when the District Council rolled out the red carpet in welcome. The photographs on these pages are taken from the official souvenir brochure.

To the
New Zealand Rugby Football Team
Visiting Newton Abbot, 1935-36

—————o—————

THIRTY years ago Newton Abbot enjoyed the honour and privilege of entertaining for their preliminary training the first representatives of the New Zealand Rugby Union that ever visited Great Britain—a team composed of players who swept everything before them on the playing field; revolutionised much of the game as we played it and earned the highest possible respect of the rugby world.

Again, in 1924, the New Zealand Rugby Union honoured us with an acceptance of our invitation, and we have many evidences that your representatives of that season shared with us the happiest recollections of their stay in our midst.

It was in the fraternal spirit of friendliness and goodwill that Newton Abbot sent its third invitation and its acceptance is regarded as an appreciation of the earlier welcomes that we have been happy to afford. It serves, moreover, as an incentive to make ourselves worthy of the honour you pay us.

Time is the true test of friendship. Thirty years is a long span and within that span we have witnessed a world-wide upheaval and many things calculated to detract our attention, yet Newton Abbot has not forgotten its friends "The All Blacks," by which title the New Zealand Rugby Footballers are always affectionately remembered.

Your visit is this town's great pleasure. Before your stay is over we sincerely hope it will be your pleasure also and that it will be proved not by words, but by happy contacts and actions, that the friendly ties of the past will be maintained and strengthened.

We welcome you to Newton Abbot and Devon, and wish you the best of luck throughout your tour, confident that you will teach us much of the great game of "Rugger" and maintain the proud traditions of your predecessors.

H.T.L.

Reception Committee waiting to greet the All Blacks. The New Zealand team later sent silver lapel badges to the committee.

New Zealand Rugby Football Team. 1935-36

Photos with acknowledgements to "The Auckland Weekly News," New Zealand.

	G. Gilbert	G. F. Hart	N. J. Ball	
H. E. Brown	N. A. Mitchell	C. J. Oliver (Vice Captain)	T. H. C. Caughey	
E. W. Tindill	D. Solomon	J. L. Griffiths	J. R. Page	
B. S. Sadler	M. M. N. Corner	A. Lambourn	W. E. Hadley	

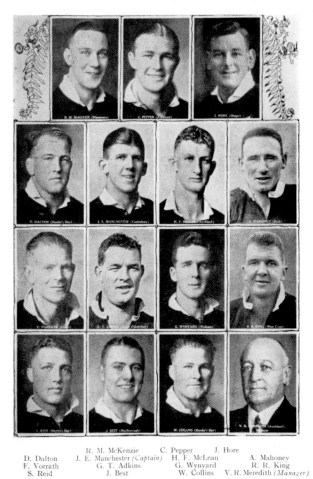

	R. M. McKenzie	C. Pepper	J. Hore	
D. Dalton	J. E. Manchester (Captain)	H. F. McLean	A. Mahoney
F. Vorrath	G. T. Adkins	G. Wynyard	R. R. King
S. Reid	J. Best	W. Collins	V. R. Meredith (Manager)

Left: Programme of Hospitality.

Right: The All Blacks training at Newton Abbot.

Programme of Hospitality

Sept.

5—Team arrives at Newton Abbot at 7 p.m. and will be officially welcomed to the Town by the Chairman of the Newton Abbot Urban District Council, Councillor Leonard Coombe, J.P.

During their stay our guests are hon. members of the Newton Abbot (Stover) Golf Club and the Constitutional, Liberal and Courtenay Clubs.

The use of the Swimming Bath and the Recreation Ground, free of charge, are also at their disposal.

6—Visit to Primley Zoological and Botanical Gardens, Paignton, at the invitation of Herbert Whitley, Esq., who will entertain the guests to tea. Leave Newton Abbot 2.30 p.m.

7—South Devon Hunt Gymkhana at Hound Tor, Dartmoor, at 2 p.m.

Dinner and Presentation of Cups to the Team and Officials at the Globe Hotel, Newton Abbot, at 8 p.m.

8—Sunday (Free).

9—Trip over Dartmoor. Leaving Newton Abbot at 10.30 a.m. to Ashburton, Buckfast Abbey, Holne, Newbridge, Poundsgate, to Dartmeet to lunch, then to Two Bridges, Princetown, Tavistock, Lydford Gorge, Okehampton, where the party will be entertained to tea by the Mayor of Okehampton (W. B. Chammings, Esq.), returning via Moretonhampstead and Bovey Tracey.

Special Cinema Performance at the Imperial Theatre, as the guests of the Management, at 8.30 p.m.

10—Luncheon to the officials and team by the Newton Abbot Rotary Club, to be followed by a visit to the Watcombe Art Potteries, and a trip around the Marine Drive, Torquay, for tea at the Grand Hotel.

Reception Dance at Globe Hotel at 8 p.m.

11—Newton Abbot Steeplechases and Hurdle Races at 3 p.m.

12—Newton Abbot Steeplechases and Hurdle Races at 2 p.m.

Special Cinema Performance at the Alexandra Theatre, as the guests of the Management, at 8.30 p.m.

13—Visit to the Works of Messrs. J. Vicary & Sons, Ltd., Fellmongers and Woolcombers, followed by visit to the Seale-Hayne Agricultural College, where the party will be entertained to tea by the Principal (W. Henderson Hogg, Esq.)

14—Opening Match of the Tour—versus Devon and Cornwall at Devonport.

15—Sunday (Free).

16—Visitors leave Newton Abbot for Coventry.

INTO THE NEW ERA

CHAPTER 9
Picking up the Pieces

IT TOOK SOME TIME for Newton Abbot to pick up the pieces after the war. On 8 September 1945, the Devon RFU announced that only eight of the original eighty-four clubs in the county, including Paignton, Exeter and Buckfastleigh, would restart at once, although it was hoped that other clubs would follow as the season progressed. Paignton arranged a game against Seale-Hayne College, but could only muster seven players. Seale-Hayne therefore lent them four men, and they played a game of eleven a side.

On 24 August 1946, a club notice appeared: 'Invitation to old players and youngsters eager to learn the game. Practice to commence at Recreation Ground on August 27. Players asked to bring their own kit.' Thus began the club's first full season of rugby for seven years. Under the aegis of Ern Flood and Percy Hodge, a full fixture list was prepared. Among the seasoned players who were available were Sanders, Robbins, Towell, Woodley, Crout, Simmonds, and of course Arthur Kift. There were still problems, however; rationing was still in place, and clothing coupons were hard to come by, so obtaining kit was difficult. One of the casualties of the war was Newton College, which could be described as the mother of rugby in the town, which closed in 1940, never to reopen.

The first match at Newton for five years was against Paignton, who had managed to keep playing throughout the war, which Newton won 10–3 in front of an enthusiastic crowd. In their second match, they beat Somerset Police 8–3, and in their third they scored another win, this time over Devonport Services, 21–12. This game featured W. Veale, who was described as 'brilliant as ever, but with all his old eccentricities'. They went on to draw 9–all against Plymouth Albion, beat Exeter 3–0 and beat Torquay 15–6. In their last match of the season, they beat Brixham 11–3. All in all, in terms of results, 1946/7 was a very satisfying season for the club. Attendances were well up, with crowds of 1,500 and 2,000 not uncommon, and the First XV won all their home games, and ended the season with a record of: played 31, won 23, drawn 2, lost 6, points for 404, points against 185. Sanders alone scored 166 points, and played for Devon against Gloucestershire.

Trouble was brewing in other areas, however. In July 1946, Newton Abbot Urban District Council had acquired the Recreation Ground from its private owners, with the aim of using it as a sports ground for the benefit of the local community. They allowed the rugby club to resume its tenancy on an annual basis, but this arrangement was not to last long. At the time, no one was to know that the match against Brixham was not only the last of the season, but the last at the Recreation Ground.

In June 1947, Newton Spurs Football Club, under the chairmanship of Major Butler, made a bid for joint use of the ground with the rugby club. However, it was felt that joint use was not practical, and the rugby club countered with an offer to buy the ground for £8,000, which was rejected. They then offered to pay an increased rent of £175, with three years paid in advance. Spurs made an even higher offer, however, and the relevant council committee recommended acceptance. Percy Hodge, who was a councillor, made a spirited plea for rugby, citing the club's long tenancy and their service to the youth of the town. He also said out that Spurs had already advertised for players from outside Newton, offering them 'first-class accomm-odation'. He also pointed out that, although Spurs had offered a higher rent for three years, once they were in residence they could name their own terms for any future tenancy; if they asked for a rent reduction, there would be little the council could do – a prophecy that turned out to be true. He therefore tabled an amendment that the rugby club should remain tenants with an increased rent for twelve months while they sought a new ground, if necessary with both clubs sharing the Recreation Ground in the meantime. This amendment was defeated by eight votes to seven. The Council Chairman, Mr A.H.W. Edworthy, a strong rugby supporter, did not record a vote; had he done so, the amendment would have been carried.

The decision resulted in a great deal of controversy, and there was a strong feeling in the town that the All Whites had been given a rough deal. There were dozens of letters to the local press, including one expressing a 'predominant feeling of disgust and nausea' adding that the Council's decision had resulted in 'a contempt quite unutterable'.

The club was therefore faced with a stark choice between finding a new ground – and quickly, as the new season was fast approaching – or giving up. They asked for a portion of an industrial site in Forde Road, but the Council refused to grant a lease. They did say they would allow the site to be used as a temporary expedient, but the club refused; they needed a proper home, otherwise the problem would simply be delayed. Two months before the new season began, therefore, fixtures had been arranged but there was no ground on which to play them, nor any changing accommodation. Despite their success in their first season after the war, the club was still a long way from resuming normal service.

At the last minute, on 6 September 1947, the Committee was able to announce that a new ground had been found, at a place called Rackerhayes, opposite the club's original ground at Teign Marshes, on land leased from quarrying company Watts, Blake & Bearne, whose Chairman, John Watts, was a great sportsman and rugby enthusiast. It had a pond alongside, which was described by a local journalist as 'a receptacle for rugby balls' and as 'offering the opportunity of a free dip for any recalcitrant referees'. He also said that only a botanist could give a name to the splendid herbage that covered the site.

The first game at the new ground took place on 22 September, against Somerset Police. Newton lost 11–3, but it was a happy occasion, and the match was played before a capacity crowd. The team was captained by veteran Eddie Elliott, and nearly all the old guard were there, including Bob Sharp, Dick Paddon, Percy Hodge, Jimmy Sharp and George Cowley. Because of the late start to the season, some of the Newton players had started playing for neighbouring clubs, but most loyally returned to their old club as soon as the new ground was ready. One notable exception was 'Shoppy' Sanders, who had moved to Torquay and decided to stay there. Nevertheless that season's team was a colourful one, with another veteran, 'Dacco' Veale playing at full back at the age of forty-three, the half-back pair of Kift and Sims, Peter Thorning, dashing 'Doc' Emmett, the big wing, Denver Baglow and the hard-tackling Ivor Murrin.

Newton also lost 11–8 to Plymouth Albion in their third game of that season, but again were supported by a rousing crowd. Two new players turned out for the Reserves, who were talked about as future stars: Ivor Murrin and Roy Stevens. Indeed, Murrin went on to play for the First XV against Torquay at Rackerhayes on 18 October, where he had an outstanding game. In that match, 'Shoppy' Sanders played for his new club against his old and missed two kickable penalties, to the accompaniment of loud cheers. The day ended tragically, however, when Bob Glanville, one of the Reserves players, received a knock in his match in Torquay, and died in his car on the way home.

That season also saw the emergence of Cliff Bowen, son of a Devon full back. He was due to play for the Juniors on the same day as the First XV were playing Somerset Police. Finding that they were one man short, the seniors roped him in at the last moment. He showed such courage and audacity against mighty forwards like the Welsh internationals Steer and Davies, that even the Police team applauded him as he left the field. He went on to even greater glory. After only one season with the First XV he was chosen for a county trial. He continued to play for the Firsts for several years, and eventually won county selection. Over seven years, he played for Devon forty times, including the team that narrowly lost the County Championship final to Middlesex in 1956 and the one that beat Yorkshire in the 1957 final. He became the youngest ever life member of the club, an honour bestowed while he was still playing. In the 1948/9 season, the team managed twenty-three wins against fifteen losses, a good record considering that the club was still to a certain extent picking up the pieces after the war and their loss of the Recreation Ground. Gordon Emmett scored eighty-four points, and Ivor Murrin ran in seventeen tries. The following season started with two superb matches against two ever-popular touring sides, Public School Wanderers and Welsh Academicals, and continued in similar vein. The increasing prominence of the club in Devon rugby was reflected in the election of Percy Hodge, for forty years the 'Mr Rugby' of Newton Abbot as President of the Devon RFU, and the selection of Ivor Murrin and Arthur Kift for the Devon team that won the South-Western Championship. Centre G. Emmett and hooker G.G. Maunder also played for the county during that season.

Cliff Bowen photographed aged 27 when playing for Devon against Yorkshire in the County Championship Final at Plymouth in 1957. He first appeared for Newton Abbot when aged 17 and later captained the side.

With the new start at Rackerhayes in 1947, Pat Hoare and Arthur Shobrook volunteered to start a Junior XV. Captained by K. Pollard, they played their first game on 11 October. So, for the first time for many years, three teams were turning out each week: the First XV, the Reserves and the Juniors.

At the AGM in 1947, Harry Bartlett, who had captained the All Whites in the previous century, proposed that the Supporters' Club be revived. This was agreed and Mrs Rayment became Chairman, with Alec Bearne as Secretary. They immediately became busy with fund-raising activities including providing chairs for the matches, programmes, draws and other fund-raising activities. Within a month the club had 161 members and had collected £183. A special appeal for funds in 1947 managed to raise another £215.

CHAPTER 10

Rackerhayes

AS WE HAVE SEEN (see Chapter 9), the Rackerhayes site was not immediately suitable for use as a rugby pitch. A lot of hard work was needed to get it ready for the coming season, and its development into a suitable ground for a club of the stature of Newton Abbot took a number of years. Its situation was ideal: the surroundings were very pleasant, it had a sandy subsoil and was fairly flat, and it was conveniently positioned between Newton Abbot and Kingsteignton. But that was all that could be said for it; it was uneven, one corner needed to be raised, and it was covered with enormous thistles, to which the club members who buckled down to clear it gave some very unbotanical names!

A Ground Improvement Fund was established, and volunteers put in a total of over 4,000 hours of labour. Some 2,400 square yards of turf were cut, 550 tons of earth were dug out to level the pitch, hundreds of tons of timber were brought in to provide temporary terraces and changing rooms, and the ground was enclosed with galvanised iron. The Committee is listed here in full to record their involvement: President John Watts, Chairman Hugh Mills, Secretary Ern Flood, Assistant Secretary H. Horrell, Treasurer C.H. Harris, members W. Davies, T. Emmett, C. Frost, A.H. Stabb, P. Hodge, W.Jones, V. Pollard, H. Shobrook, J.E. Evans, A. Shobrook, C.A. Jackson, C. Scott and W. Warren. The two builders, High Mills and Alec Bearne, were obviously to the fore, as was Charlie Scott, who gave a great deal to the club before his sudden departure a few years later. Players and ordinary members also helped.

Further developments took place during the summer of 1948, when the Supporters' Club used the money they had raised to erect two excellent dressing rooms, with baths, a referee's room and a boiler room. The plaque over the door read, 'To the glory of sport and the future of rugby.' On 18 September the Supporters' Club President, Mrs W. Davies handed the new building over to the club President, Mr John Watts.

This was also the date of the official opening of the ground, even though it had been in use for most of the previous season. The event was attended by a number of dignitaries, including officials from the Devon RFU, local authority VIPs and the local MP, Brigadier Sir Ralph Rayner. Rosslyn Park RFC made a special trip from London with a team that included two internationals and eight county players to play a celebration match against Newton, which the home side lost 29–6.

More developments followed in 1951, with the completion of a 300-seater grandstand, built by volunteer labour. A temporary outer enclosure of corrugated iron was erected in the same year, as well a concrete post and rail fence around the playing area. Rackerhayes was beginning to look like a ground fit for a club of the stature to which Newton Abbot aspired.

The next phase of development took place in 1956. Despite the club's difficult general financial position, the appeal for funds to provide a memorial to the late Percy Hodge was successful enough for the building of a new clubhouse in his memory to commence. Built by A.G. Bearne Builders, it boasted a new, and potentially lucrative, feature – a licensed bar. The Percy Hodge Memorial Clubhouse was opened by the President of the Devon RFU, Mr E.R.B. Stanbury, on 29 March. The occasion was marked by a match between Devon and a South Devon XV, in which Cliff Bowen played at full back for Devon and his brother, Maurice at full back for South Devon. Thanks to the help of the Supporters' Club, the club managed to clear the whole of the debt incurred in the building of the clubhouse by 1960.

In 1960, too, a club benefactor, who wished to remain anonymous at the time but can now be revealed as Dr D.J. Bannerman, made a gift of a scoreboard. He was once heard to comment: 'I thought I knew something about rugby, but indeed, these lady supporters have taught me a lot!' It was also decided to plant 120 poplar trees on the pond side of the ground. The cost of the trees, at 12s 6d each, was raised by the ingenious method of painting pictures of the trees on a sheet of card and inviting individuals and teams to write their name under one, and thus commit to 'buying a tree'.

These developments were followed in 1961 by an ambitious five-year plan, which included tarring the road to the ground, building a wall and entrance gates, replacing the corrugated iron fence with chain-link and filling in the marshy ground at the Kingsteignton end to provide another pitch. In 1961, the Juniors also built their own dressing rooms.

A couple of years later, there was an approach from some greyhound racing promoters for a track round the pitch. This would have been a very profitable venture for the club, but unfortunately it did not materialise.

A new twenty-eight-year lease for the ground was negotiated with Watts, Blake & Bearne in 1964, giving the club some security for the future. Following the death of Percy Hodge's widow, a bequest of £360 came to the club, and it was agreed that it should go towards the building of a new and bigger clubhouse. Meanwhile, the five-year plan was coming to fruition, with the building of an attractive wall at the Newton Abbot end of the ground by a few volunteers led by Phil McCue, who was awarded the Chris Wakeham Trophy, the erection of cast-iron gates and the replacement of the corrugated iron boundary with chain-link fencing.

It was decided to apply for grants through the Devon Playing Fields Association and the local authority towards the estimated £12,000 cost of the remaining element of the five-year plan, the filling in, levelling and seeding of the ground at the Kingsteignton end to provide further pitches, together with the erection of a new clubhouse. A government grant of £3,800 was promised, enabling the latter project to go ahead. Designed by Treasurer George Bowden, the clubhouse was built in just ten weeks, largely through the voluntary efforts of players and members of the committee. The old clubhouse, linked to the new, was converted into a kitchen and dining room. The combined building, like its simpler predecessor, was named after Percy Hodge, whose bequest had contributed to the costs.

In considering who should open the new clubhouse, the committee rather cheekily invited the Minister of Sport, Denis Howells, together with Harlequins, probably the most famous club in England. To everyone's amazement and delight, both accepted. Thus, on 2 September 1967, Mr Howells unveiled a plaque to open the building. Also present were representatives of Devon RFU and the Chairmen of the Newton Abbot Urban and Rural District Councils. The ceremony was followed by a match against Harlequins, which the latter won by the narrowest of margins, 6–5, despite consisting entirely of county players, including four internationals.

The new developments had been helped along by the government grant, and by a £3,000 loan from the RFU. The club now sought help from the local authority; it was the only club in South Devon not to be supported in some way by its local authority. They asked for help with the transport of the thousands of tons of filling material needed to fill in the marshy ground that had been earmarked for new pitches. The Urban District Council agreed to provide £3,000 at £300 per year for ten years. The Supporters' Club and Social Club presented the club with cheques totalling £1,400 in 1969, and loan bonds were issued – non-interest-bearing loans to be repaid after fifteen years. In the event, few people claimed repayment. The filling material was donated by Lord Clifford, so the club only had to pay for the transport.

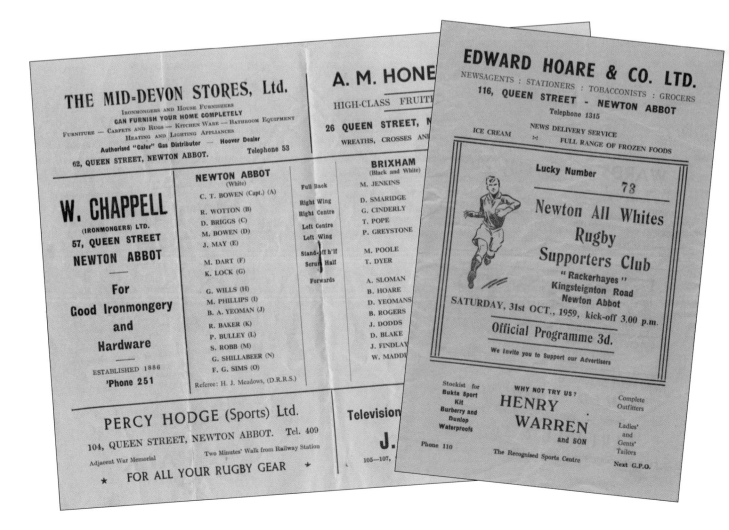

CHAPTER 11

The Passing of the Old Guard

THE NEW DECADE started with a bang. Joint Secretary Major Evans had persuaded mighty Cardiff to send a team especially to play Newton Abbot, and they duly arrived on 18 September 1950. They were greeted by the largest crowd ever seen in Rackerhayes's short history, and ended a thrilling game only just victorious, 6–3. Newton had a new young fly half in Dave Singer, who acquitted himself against his opposite number, a certain Cliff Morgan, who was playing his first game for Cardiff. Morgan, of course, went on to carve out a niche for himself as one of the 'immortals' of international rugby. The game was followed by a dinner at the Courtenay Restaurant, followed by a ball, during which the Cardiff players treated their hosts to some of their moving songs.

Cardiff were followed by another famous Welsh side, Aberavon, who were touring the West Country. Having beaten Exeter and Torquay, they managed only a draw against Newton Abbot, 3–all. Indeed, the season as a whole produced some superb games. In addition to the visits from Cardiff and Aberavon, there were drawn games against Old Blues and an international-studded Public School Wanderers and – the game of the season – a 14–13 loss against Welsh Academicals.

The following season produced only moderate success, with victories over Plymouth Albion, Torquay, Penryn and Barnstaple, although the Juniors won the Haarer Cup in the Devon Seven-a-Side Championship. The First XV recovered in 1952/3, however, with their best season since moving to Rackerhayes. They lost only twelve games out of forty-two, with 337 points for and 166 against. Their record included 'double' wins against Plymouth Albion, Paignton, Barnstaple, Exmouth, RNE College and Brixham. Top scorers in this season were Ralph Daw and Arthur Kift, with fifty-one points each – Daw's from kicks and Kift's from a mixture of tries and kicks.

Several promising new young players were beginning to make their mark in the early 1950s: Cliff Bowen, who was performing like a seasoned First XV player despite his youth, Ron Mudge, Graham Camm, a tricky wing who went on to represent Devon, Frank Sims, a convert from football, and Dave Newbury, who proved himself a worthy successor to Arthur Kift's former scrum-half partner Mickey Sims. He was, however, challenged for this position by Ken 'Topsy' Lock, who eventually made the position his own. He was soon looking for a new fly-half partner; Arthur Kift, after many years of inspiring leadership and skilful service, to both Newton Abbot and Devon, announced his retirement in 1953.

Klift's departure seemed to unsettle the team, which faced a formidable fixture list for the 1953/4 season, including Public School Wanderers, the Metropolitan Police, Pontypool, Aberavon and a Pembrokeshire county XV. They beat Public School Wanderers, the Police team and Pembrokeshire, but lost to Pontypool and Aberavon. Locally they beat Torquay once and Plymouth Albion, but their overall record was somewhat mixed: seventeen games lost out of thirty-seven. However, one bright spot was the selection of Cliff Bowen for Devon and Cornwall in a match against the All Blacks. In 1955, in addition to the usual crop of powerful visitors (including Headingly, Pontypool, Newbridge, Aberavon, Cardiff and Pembrokeshire) Newton also played host to a team from HMNZS Bellona, which was based in Plymouth, beating them 9–6 in January and losing to them 11–5 in April.

It was not only the players who were changing. Ern Flood, who had held or shared the post of Secretary for over thirty years, retired in 1951, although he remained on the committee. Harry Shobrook, who had given years of service as Treasurer, also stepped down in that year, and a number of other club stalwarts, including Harry Frost, Sam Wyatt, Bob Sharp and George Stephens, died that year. The following year, Mr C.L. Vicary, for many years club and county President, died, as did Harry Shobrook and V. Pollard, both ex-Treasurers. These deaths were followed in 1954 by that of Percy Hodge, who had served the club and Devon for over fifty years, as player, committee member and office holder. Charles Frost retired as Secretary the same year. It seemed like a changing of the guard, the end of an era.

The Supporters' Club continued with their fund-raising efforts; over their first four years, they raised almost £2,000 for the club, and in 1951 they started a Kingsteignton branch. However, the financial situation was not promising; like many clubs, Newton Abbot suffered a drop in income as television became popular as a form of entertainment, and in 1955 called a meeting of South Devon clubs to see what could be done about it. In the meantime a fund was opened to pay for a fitting memorial for Percy Hodge, and as it turned out that provided one solution to the problem.

The club achieved a degree of fame when it was featured in *The Tatler and Bystander* of 3 October 1951, as part of their 'Famous Rugby Club' series.

CHAPTER 12

Controversy and Tragedy

THE CLUB HAD a good season in 1956/7, as did the county. Newton were unbeaten for six months, and scored victories over Plymouth Albion, Torquay Athletic, Penzance-Newlyn, Camborne, Falmouth and Exeter, as well as first-time visitors Streatham-Croydon. Devon, moreover, became County Champions for the first time since 1912, and the seventh time in their history, by beating Yorkshire in Plymouth 12–3. Newton Abbot's Cliff Bowen had an excellent game at full back, and was singled out for special praise by Jeff Butterfield, the Yorkshire (and England) captain at the post-match dinner.

Charlie Scott

The following season was also fairly successful, with just thirteen defeats out of forty-three played. One of those defeats, however, was by a massive 60–25, against St Luke's College. Newton gained their revenge, however, in the return match, at Rackerhayes. Newton won a historic victory 9–3, bringing to an end St Luke's incredible run of a season and a half without a loss. The match was not without incident. As St Luke's threw everything into trying to maintain their record towards the end of the match, one of their players, Howard Morris, was sent off, soon followed by Ken Simmonds of Newton Abbot, and then by Charlie Scott – who was only the touch judge! Double victories were recorded over Paignton, Brixham and Teignmouth. The 1958/9 season also saw centre Maurice Bowen score a club record 193 points.

1959 saw the arrival of a team of US Marines. Stationed in London, they were accommodated at the Royal Signals Regiment barracks at Denbury. Tickets for the match were pre-sold for several weeks before it was noticed that they referred to Newton's opponents as 'the US Royal Marines'. Embarrassingly, the News of the World picked up on the fact that the Queen had apparently retaken the American colonies, so the mistake made national news. However, one good thing came out of it – the publicity probably boosted ticket sales, and a very good crowd turned out. Newton won easily by thirty points. The marines were presented with inscribed blue mugs from Dartmouth Pottery.

Another visiting team in the same year was Chairman John Evans's old club, Tenby, from Wales. Major Evans assumed that the team had not improved significantly since his time there as a youth, and advised Newton to take it easy after the first twenty points. What he had not realised was that Tenby had brought together a number of 'exile' players. In consequence they won 9–6 without Newton having to take it easy. Indeed, the bloodied team held it against their Chairman for many years afterwards!

The club soon found itself embroiled in a major controversy. Cliff Bowen, the prize player, loyal club member, Captain and son of a superb former player, completed forty games for Devon at full back in the 1959/60 season, and was made the youngest ever life member. However, that same season saw the return from National Service of Stuart Morris, son of Sid Morris, who had given a lifetime of service to the club, and his wife, who was Treasurer of the Kingsteignton branch of the Supporters' Club. He had grown up 100 yards from Rackerhayes, and had practised his kicking there. While on National Service, he had progressed from playing for his unit to Aldershot Services, the Army and Hampshire, and was being touted as a potential future international full back. On his return to Newton in the middle of the season, however, he found Cliff Bowen firmly ensconced in his favourite position in the First XV – and, moreover, as Captain of the team. The selectors were therefore faced with a dilemma: whether to choose the long-serving, loyal Captain and full back in situ, despite the fact that he was probably nearing the end of his career, or the rising young star with international potential.

The problem was painfully resolved at a full meeting of the whole committee and the players. The Chairman made a plea to those present: 'Individual players come and go, the club goes on. Before reaching a decision you must ask yourselves one question: what is best for the club?' The final decision was that Morris should be the one. It was not a universally popular decision, but it had at least been democratically arrived at. In the meantime, Torquay tried to take advantage of Newton's dilemma by sending a delegation to Morris, offering him the chance to play for them. He did, indeed, play a few games for them, but his heart was in Newton Abbot and he returned to the All Whites the following season. He served the club for many years, and continued to play for Hampshire for a time before switching to Devon. He was a reserve for the England team on several occasions, and played for the Barbarians on their Easter tour of South Wales in 1964.

The Devon RFU side in 1955/6 with Newton Abbot player Cliff Bowen (playing at fullback), seen second row from front, third from left.

The fallout from the controversy continued into the following year, when Cliff Bowen's brother Maurice and Bob Wotton left the club in protest at the decision. Fortunately, both later returned. Others also left, and the 1960/1 season saw the introduction of a number of new, younger players into the side. The club's policy was not to bring in players from elsewhere, with the result that a number of Reserves now made it into the First XV, including winger Alan Kennard and centre Chris Wakeham. The new team grew in confidence, but in the meantime experienced a series of unspectacular seasons.

The team was briefly strengthened by the arrival in 1959 of John Hancock, a Captain in the Royal Signals Regiment stationed at Denbury. He had played for Harlequins for several years, as well as the Army and Combined Services. Unfortunately he returned to London the following season.

The 1962/3 season was marked by the 'big freeze', and no games could be played between Boxing Day and 16 February; training was undertaken at Goodrington Sands – a novel innovation, but neither very exciting nor very successful. Like the previous couple of years, it was a very mixed season in terms of results, with fifteen losses out of thirty-five games, but some spectacular successes. Newton beat local rivals Torquay and Plymouth Albion, but also some top-class visiting teams: London Welsh were beaten 9–3, Cheltenham 16–0, Public School Wanderers 12–6. The First XV also paid a visit to Streatham, whom they beat 8–3.

The following season saw an improvement, with only seventeen losses out of forty-five games. And in the year that his father was made a life member of the club, Stuart Morris, one of the first attacking full backs, scored seven tries, twenty-two conversions, seventeen penalties and two dropped goals, for a season's total of 122 points. It was also the year that, having already played for two counties (Hampshire and Devon) and the Army and Combined Services, as well as being a reserve for England, he was chosen for the Barbarians' tour of Wales.

In 1963, Chairman Major Evans introduced a system of club ties. The member's tie was navy blue embroidered with abbots in gold. The players' version had a similar design, but with the addition of 'XV'. There was also a merit tie, awarded to members and officials who had given outstanding service of not less than four years, and players who had completed not less than four years representing the club regularly in either the First or the Second XV. If lost, it would never be replaced.

Tragedy struck the club in 1964, with the death of the powerful centre Chris Wakeham, who was a regular First XV player and also played for Devon. Only twenty-three, he was killed by a runaway wagon in the underground section of the clay pit where he worked. A trophy for 'Clubman of the Year' was dedicated to his memory, and it was perhaps fitting that the first recipient was Roy Baker, the Captain. It was also, perhaps, fitting that his passing should be marked by one of the team's best seasons in recent times, with only thirteen losses out of forty-one games, with 670 points scored. Stuart Morris was again the top scorer, with 158 points.

That season also saw the reintroduction of a Devon seven-a-side tournament in Plymouth. Newton beat the favourites, St Luke's, in the semi-finals, but lost in the final to Plymouth Albion. Even Don Rowe, the Chairman of Exeter, was heard cheering on Newton Abbot before stopping himself with the exclamation, 'Good God, what am I doing? I never thought I'd ever cheer for Newton!'

CHAPTER 13

Ton Up!

THE CLUB NOW ENTERED a short period of increasing success. The record for the 1965/6 season was: played 46, won 34, drew 4, lost 8, points for 764, points against 239. Three players scored more than 100 points: wing Mike Scott with 111, Maurice Bowen, now returned to Newton with 144, and Stuart Morris with 133. Scott's tally came from a record thirty-seven tries, and the other wing, Ian Ballardie joined in the scoring spree with twenty-six. Altogether a record 165 tries were scored. Newton Abbot also contributed more players to the Devon team that season than any other club: Stuart Morris, John Appleyard, Phil McCue and John Perryman. Indeed the team was almost top-heavy with county players, as Scott, Ballardie, Bowen, Roy Baker and Trevor Harvey had all played for Devon. This success was largely down to strength in depth: the Second XV was a first-rate team, as was the Junior side, presided over by the uncompromising Les Tucker.

The following season was also a good one, although not quite as successful, with twenty-eight victories out of forty-three games. There were several newcomers to the club, including full back Bob White from Exeter (who scored 178 points in the 1968/9 season), replacing the injured Stuart Morris, Barry Venning, a county prop forward from Buckfastleigh, who had been playing for Paignton, and another Devon prop Harry Barnes.

Following the opening of the new clubhouse in 1967 and a narrow loss to mighty Harlequins, the team excelled themselves by beating Torquay 14–6, Penryn, one of the strongest teams in Cornwall 9–3 and two county teams no less – Hampshire 11–6 and the rest of Devon 13–12.

The strength in depth was illustrated when the First XV lost the services of Stuart Morris and Phil McCue through injury in 1968/9, as well as Dave Sutcliffe and John Appleyard, who left the district. They were replaced by teenagers Mike Admore, Philip Husband, Jim Luscombe and Alan Rogers.

The 1969/70 season saw the retirement of long-serving Secretary Ken Poat, and a new role for former Captain Roy Baker, who took over from him. It was also marked by a visit from Cardiff, including Mervyn John, the brother of the immortal Barry. The visitors won 18–8. Another arrival, this time permanent, was Terry Yabsley, who turned up one day and asked, 'What can I do to help with the coaching and administration of the Juniors?' He remained a stalwart of the club for many years, as did his wife and his son Tim, who worked his way up through the Juniors and Reserves, and ended up

Club News

THIS evening we welcome Newton Abbot who have been quite a force in Devon Rugby for the past couple of years. We hope they enjoy the game and stay with us this evening.

The Exeter side has been producing some very good attacking rugby this Season, even when they have not been at full strength. This type of Rugby does a lot of good for the game and we hope Newton Abbot will join us in throwing the ball about so as to produce an enjoyable

Programme

EXETER v NEWTON ABBOT
TUESDAY, SEPTEMBER 26th, 1967
Kick-off 5.45 p.m.

EXETER (Black)				NEWTON ABBOT	
15	R. Staddon		Full-back	15	R. White
14	G. Angel		Right Wing	14	M. Scott
13	*J. Radford	Three-quarters		13	*M. Bowen
12	M. Fisher			12	G. Arscott
11	*A. Vinnicombe		Left Wing	11	B. Leonard
10	*B. Carless		Stand off half-backs	10	M. Dart
9	*K. A. Hopper Cpt.	Scrum		9	R. Wicks
1	*G. Edmondson		Forwards	1	W. Furze
2	C. Bright			2	D. Sutcliffe
3	A. Rees			3	*H. Barnes
4	*J. Baxter			4	D. Lear
5	M. Faulkner		Referee	5	*R. Baker
6	*A. Cole		Mr. T. Hickman (D.A.R.S.)	6	W. Gilpin
8	*D. Manley			8	T. Evans Cpt.
7	M. Gardner			7	B. Hayman

* County

Next match on this ground—
SATURDAY NEXT, SEPTEMBER 30th, 1967

EXETER
v
GLAMORGAN WANDS.
Kick-off 3.15 p.m.

Refreshments . . .
on sale from the Memorial Club Room — Moderate Charges

Fixtures, 1967-68

				Result
				P F A
Sept. 2	Moseley	1967	A	L 3 16
" 4	(M.) Harlequins		A	L 8 13
" 9	Esher		H	
"	R.F.U. Canadian Tour Team v Southern Area		H	
" 16	Torquay		W	8 13
" 19	Devon v Hampshire		H	24 6
" 23	Penzance & Newlyn		A	W 26 13 0
" 26	(Tu.) Newton Abbot		H	W 34 0
" 30	Glamorgan Wands.		H	
Oct. 7	Devonport Ser.		A	
" 14	Redruth		A	
" 18	Devon v Royal Navy		H	
" 21	Saracens		H	
" 28	Clifton		A	
" 28	Devon v Glos. at Bristol			
Nov. 4	England v New Zealand			
" 11	Devon v Cornwall at Plymouth			
" 18	Exmouth		H	
" 25	Paignton		A	
" 25	Devon v Somerset at Torquay			
Dec. 2	Torquay		H	
" 9	Barnstaple		H	
" 16	London Hospital		H	
" 23	Teignmouth		H	
" 26	(Tu.) Exmouth		A	
" 30	Plymouth A.		H	
Jan. 6	Taunton	1968	H	
" 13	St. Luke's Col.		H	
" 20	Bridgwater		A	
" 27	England v Wales			
Feb. 3	Belfast R.A.F.P.		H	
" 10	Weston-super-Mare		H	
" 17	Barnstaple		A	
" 24	Guy's Hospital		H	
Mar. 2	Plymouth A.		A	
" 9	Devonport Ser.		A	
" 16	Bridgend		A	
" 19	(Tu.) St. Luke's Col.		H	
" 23	Cheltenham		H	
" 30	Old Blues		H	
April 6	(Tu.) Bristol		A	
" 13	Old Cranleighans		H	
" 15	Moseley		H	
" 20	Bath		H	
" 27	Redruth		A	
" 29	(M.) Gloucester		H	

W—Won L—Lost D—Drawn

EXETER FOOTBALL CLUB

(Affiliated to the R.F.U. and Devon R.F.U.)

COUNTY GROUND
ST. THOMAS

President .... A. PETER STEELE-PERKINS, M.C.
Chairman .... P. D. ROWSELL
Hon. Secretary .... L. J. B. CHALLENGER
'Phone 56655 (home), 75678 (office)
Hon. Treasurer .... J. N. P. RICHARDS
'Phone Shaldon 3226 (home), Exeter 77381 (office)
Teams Hon. Sec. .... R. J. PUGSLEY
Fixtures Hon. Sec. .... J. G. HARRISON Phone 55375
Captain .... K. A. HOPPER Phone 74959

SUPPORTERS' CLUB OFFICIALS:
President .... G. PRING
Chairman .... C. H. HOLDING
Hon. Secretary .... H. H. TILT
Hon. Treasurer .... K. J. C. VERCOE

Official Programme

1st XV FIXTURES 1968-69

Sept. 3	South Devon XV	H	16-11 (s)
" 6	Trojans	H	1-
" 11	Paignton	A	12-10
" 12			
" 14	Sidmouth	H	23-6
" 19	Exeter	H	23-6
" 21	Exmouth	A	34-6
" 25	Teignmouth	H	11-3
" 28	Penzance-Newlyn	H	
		A	
Oct. 5	Penryn	H	
" 12	Plymouth Albion	H	6-3
" 26	Brixham	A	
Nov. 2	Somerset Police	H	
" 6	St. Barts. Hospital	H	
" 9	Bideford	H	
" 16	Devonport Services	H	
" 23	Torquay Athletic	H	
" 30	Rhymney	H	
Dec. 7	Barnstaple	H	
" 14	Brixham	A	
" 21	Plymouth Albion	A	
" 26	South Devon Rags	H	
" 28	Teignmouth	H	

Jan. 4	Yeovil	
" 11	St. Luke's College	
" 18	Glynneath	
" 25	Hampshire	
Feb. 1	Redruth	
" 8	St. Luke's College	
" 15	Teignmouth	
" 22	Woodford	
Mar. 1	Sutton	
" 8	Tredegar	
" 15	Torquay Athletic	
" 19	B.R.N.C.	
" 22	Penryn	
" 26	Paignton	
" 29	Sidmouth	
Apr. 5	Solihull	
" 7	Leicester Reynards	
" 12	Barnstaple	
" 16	Paignton	
" 19	Somerset Police	H
" 23	Exmouth	A
" 26	Weston-super-Mare	A

PLAYERS. Last minute emergency calls to Ken Poat
(Home) 4018 (Bus.) 4118

6

7

1968-69

NEWTON ABBOT RUGBY FOOTBALL CLUB

Founded 1873

Vice-President

Season Ticket

as Chairman! His first season in charge was a good one for the Juniors, and in his second, 1970/1 they reached the semi-finals of the Devon Colts Cup.

In the same season, Newton organised the first open seven-a-side tournament since the war. It took place on 5 April and was won by Bideford, who beat Torquay 15–11 in the final.

The long-serving Chairman, Major John Evans, left the area in 1970; he was given a rousing send-off at a dinner at Rackerhayes, attended by representatives of Devon RFU and other clubs, and made a life member of the club. In the same year the club lost one of its top players, Bill Furze, who died on the pitch while playing for Devon Police in Exeter. He had come up through the Juniors, and was a very popular member – the church was packed to overflowing for his memorial service. A special match in aid of his family was played on 8 March between teams from Mid Devon and Torbay. A trophy was created in his memory to reward the most promising Colts player, and the first recipient, in 1971, was Doug Brown.

There was some talk of merging the All Whites and Teignmouth in 1972 to form a 'Teignbridge' club based at Rackerhayes. Although it was accepted that such a merger might become necessary at some stage, the feeling was that it was better to remain independent for the foreseeable future.

After twenty years of service, the Supporters' Club was incorporated into the main club Committee in 1970.

After a succession of successful seasons, the run-up to the club's centenary was disappointing. The First XV started 1970/1 well, with six victories out of seven, but then faded. In the following season they won just fourteen of their forty-four matches; no fewer than forty-five players turned out for the First XV at various times during the season! In 1972/3 they managed to win twenty-one, including six out of eight against South Devon rivals.

And so dawned the centenary season. It would be nice to record that the club celebrated with a succession of wins, but sadly it was not to be. The record read: played 39, won 13, drew 2, lost 24, points for 468, points against 716. A special centenary match was played against old friends Public School Wanderers, who arrived with ten international players and proceeded to beat their hosts 50–16 in a highly entertaining game. Another celebration match, against Devon, also ended in defeat, 34–3. The centenary dinner was attended by the RFU President Mickey Steele-Bodger, the founder of the Public School Wanderers, Charles Burton and Dr F. Dwyer, President of the Devon RFU. Another highlight of the centenary season was a visit by a party of New Zealand supporters, who recalled the great days when the All Blacks made Newton Abbot their headquarters.

Above: 1946/47

Left: Supporter's Club
President W. Davies receiving
a presentation c.1950

Below: 1951/52

c.1950

c.1950

1949-50

1949/50

1949/50

c.1950

1952-53

Newton Abbot Blues, 1950

1952-53

Devon v All Blacks

1953-54

1954-55

Newton Abbot at Teignmouth c.1955

1955-56

1957-58

1958-59

c.1958

1962-63

1962-63

mid 1960s

mid 1960s

1st. XV FIXTURES

September 1966
Thurs.	1	Public School Wanderers	(H)
Wed.	7	Brixham	
Sat.	10	Barnstaple	(A)
Thurs.	15	Exeter	(A)
Sat.	17	Somerset Police	(H)
Wed.	21	Teignmouth	(H)
Sat.	24	Penzance-Newlyn	(H)

October
Sat.	1	Southend	(H)
Sat.	8	Plymouth Albion	(H)
Sat.	15	Paignton	(H)
Sat.	22	Exmouth	(A)
Sat.	29	St. Luke's College	(H)

November
Sat.	5	Truro	
Wed.	9	St. Bart's Hospital	(H)
Sat.	12	Somerset Police	(H)
Sat.	19	Devonport Services	(A)
Sat.	26	Torquay Ath.	(H)

December
Sat.	3	Britannia R.N.C.	(H)
Sat.	10	Sutton	(A)
Sat.	17	Plymouth Albion	(H)
Sat.	31	Winchester	(A)

January 1967
Sat.	7	Exmouth	(H)
Sat.	14	Woodford	(A)
Sat.	21	Barnstaple	(H)
Sat.	28	Paignton	(H)

1st. XV FIXTURES

February
Sat.	4	Teignmouth	(A)
Sat.	11	Exeter University	(A)
Sat.	18	St. Luke's College	(A)
Sat.	25	Bristol University	(H)

March
Sat.	4	Exeter University	(H)
Sat.	11	Sidmouth	(H)
Sat.	18	Hampshire XV	(H)
Sat.	22	Britannia R.N.C.	(H)
Sat.	25	Old Dixonians	(H)
Mon.	27	C.H. Old Edwardians	(H)

April
Sat.	1	Sidmouth	
Wed.	5	Torquay Ath.	(A)
Sat.	8	Yeovil	(A)
Wed.	12	Brixham	(H)
Fri.	14	Glynneath	(H)
Sat.	22	Weston-s-Mare	(A)
Mon.	24	*Cardiff	(A)
Sat'	29	Penryn	(A)

* All Pay Match

NEWTON ABBOT ALL WHITES SUPPORTERS CLUB

SEASON 1966—67

VICE-PRESIDENT

....

---

22 MID-DEVON ADVERTISER, SATURDAY, JANUARY, 31, 1970

WHITES MASTER THE MUDBATH

All Whites 9pts, Yeovil 3

RUGBY IS never the same when it is played in torrential rain and on a mudbath of a pitch. There is little room for open play or for individual skill.

It is not surprising, therefore, that this match produced no star performers or many bright moments. The players probably found it just as easy throwing the ball around the showers after the match as they did throwing the ball around during the game.

But both sides tried to keep the game open. They rarely indulged in aimless kicking into touch and only once did they try their hand at soccer tactics.

The only difference between the two sides was the fact that All Whites had a reliable kicker whereas Yeovil did not.

It was 16-year-old winger Phil Loder who provided the lethal boot. He missed an early penalty chance but after ten minutes had better luck when he converted an attempt from 30 yards.

Fifteen minutes later he was on target again from in front of the posts.

Both kicks were good considering the conditions. Yeovil's lock forward and captain John Burgess proved that kicking was by no means easy when he missed a penalty from 20 yards.

Wing-forward Simon Day put All Whites further ahead before half-time when he snapped up a half-chance on the Yeovil line, slipped through the defence and dived over near the corner.

Burgess made up for his earlier miss when two minutes into the second half he converted a penalty. But despite their willingness to attack Yeovil were unable to pierce the solid All Whites rearguard.

The match will be remembered more for the atrocious conditions rather than for the quality of play. Both sides deserve credit, however, for attempting to keep the game open. Had it been played on a firm pitch there might have been some exciting rugby.

All Whites: M. Dart; ......more, M. Scott, R. Ice, ... V. Hosking, M. Lewis, R. Yeaning, A. Rogers, I. McLean, T. Harvey, N. Tapper, S. Day, D. Lear, J. Luscombe.

Yeovil: J. Denning; F. March, G. Sabran, G. Holland, B. Gamblin; A...... Graham, G. Thomas; M. Biss, J. Thouless, D. Price, A. Bowers, T. Stevens, S. Maunder, J. Burgess, P. Hempstead.

ABOVE: All Whites' scrum-half Mike Lewis receives the ball from a lineout during the match between All Whites and Yeovil. **BELOW:** Drenched to the skin with mud and rain, forwards take a breather before a lineout. The match, played at Rackerhayes in appalling conditions, was won by All Whites by nine points to six. Towards the end it became difficult to identify the players as their blue and black shirts became covered with mud.

Rugby

NEWTON ABBOT RUGBY FOOTBALL CLUB

You are invited to play for the *Colts* XV against *Exeter Univ*

on Saturday *23.11.08* at *Home* ground.

K.O. *1 45* p.m. Coach leaves ....

IF UNABLE TO PLAY PLEASE NOTIFY *N.H. 4018*

and Nicholls IMMEDIATELY

Memo. *Please tell Easterbrook^ that he is playing — Feasby is reserve.*

NEWTON ABBOT RUGBY FOOTBALL CLUB

You are invited to play for the *Colts* XV against *Exeter Saracens*

on Saturday *15 FEB 1969* at *NEWTON ABBOT* ground.

K.O. *2-00* p.m. Coach leaves ....

IF UNABLE TO PLAY PLEASE NOTIFY *N.A. 4018*

Memo. *Please ask Feasby to come as reserve.* IMMEDIATELY

1965-66

Newton Abbot
Rugby Football Club

Founded 1873

SEASON 1976-77

SATURDAY, 31st JANUARY, 1970
K.O. 3.8 p.m.

NEWTON ABBOT		REDRUTH
M. DART (15)	Full Back	M. DOWNING (15)
M. CUDMORE (14)	Right Wing	J. RICHARDS (14)
I. COOPER (13)	Right Centre	R. GEORGE (Capt) (13)
S. ARNOLD (12)	Left Centre	M. SWEENEY (12)
P. LODER (11)	Left Wing	J. MILLS (11)
V. HOSKINGS (10)	Stand-off	D. YELLAND (10)
M. LEWIS (9)	Scrum	P. SWEENEY (9)
R. TOWELL (1)	Forwards	R. BUCKINGHAM (1)
A. ROGERS (2)		P. KINSEY (2)
B. VENNING (3)		C. R. JOHNS (3)
N. TAPPER (4)		T. BUZZA (4)
T. HARVEY (Capt.) (5)		M. TAYLOR (5)
S. DAY (6)		R. PRYOR (6)
D. LEAR (8)		T. TONKIN (8)
J. LUSCOMBE (7)		K. PORTER (7)

We welcome Redruth to Rackerhayes and hope that they enjoy their visit. This fixture, which commenced over 60 years ago, has produced some first-class displays of Rugby and we hope today's game is no exception.

We are hoping to arrange our cup fixture against St. Luke's College for a Sunday, possibly February 15.

FOOTBALL COMPETITION — NEW MEMBERS WELCOME

CONFECTIONER   TOBACCONIST
NEWSAGENT

W. G. ROWELL

ICE CREAM   KUNZLE CAKES
GIFTS

74, QUEEN STREET
NEWTON ABBOT (Phone 3821)

Also Market Square & Omnibus Stn.
NEWTON ABBOT, Devon

THOMAS ELLIOT
(BAKERS) LTD.

HOME-MADE
BREAD, CAKES and PASTRIES
at Best Possible Value

BED and BREAKFAST

34, WOLBOROUGH STREET
NEWTON ABBOT.   Tel. 4528

1970

1977

1978/79

c.1979/80

1979

1979/80

mid 1980s

Menu

Cream of Chicken Soup

———

Roast Sirloin of Beef with Yorkshire Pudding
Roast and Creamed Potatoes
Cauliflower with White Sauce
Vichy Carrots

———

Sherry Trifle with Cream
or
Peach Melba

———

Cheese and Biscuits
Coffee

Toast List

THE QUEEN
Proposed by B. Loder, Esq., Chairman, N.A.R.F.C.

———

NEWTON ABBOT R.F.C.
Proposed by W. J. C. Watts, Esq., President N.A.R.F.C.

Response by R. S. Burgin, Esq., Captain N.A.R.F.C.

———

Presentation of Awards by Mrs. Watts

NEWTON ABBOT RUGBY FOOTBALL CLUB

ANNUAL DINNER
and DANCE

Friday, 9th May, 1980

LANGSTONE CLIFF HOTEL
DAWLISH WARREN

mid 1980s

1985/86

1987/88

THE MODERN ERA

CHAPTER 14
The Journey Continues

THE CLUB'S DECLINE was halted by the RFU's introduction of the National League structure in 1987, which brought an end to the traditional system of friendly fixtures. The change in format initially gave Newton an uncomfortable reality check, but then went on to provide solid foundations for the future, which have seen the club move from Devon One to National Three in twelve years, from a men only sport to one which gladly involves families, children, girls and ladies teams.

During the good times the All Whites were a force to be reckoned with, boasting an impressively strong fixture list that had been built up and maintained as the club became one of the most highly regarded sides in the south-west. However the momentum slowed as both playing numbers and the quality of personnel declined. But the strong fixture list was still in place, which resulted in one particularly unmemorable season when only two matches were won.

The starting position of each club for the inaugural National League season, 1987/8, was determined by a combination of fixture list, results and geographical location. These factors combined to put Newton in the Cornwall and Devon Division from where, after another poor season, the club suffered – for the first and only time – relegation into Devon One, the lowest tier at the time. This was an ignominious position for a club that had over the years mixed it with the best in the west and even further afield. They now found themselves pitted against clubs that were only on their Second XV fixture list before the League era.

However, this seemed to shake the club up, and from then on Newton experienced near continuous success at whatever level they played. Top-half finishes have been the norm, with promotion nearly always on the cards. The club's only demotion came at the end of that season. Nevertheless, it was not until 1998 that promotion was actually gained, when Newton became Champions of Devon One after several seasons of just losing out. A second successive elevation followed as the team became Champions of Cornwall and Devon in their first season and moved into the Western Counties Division.

Over the subsequent twelve seasons steady progress was made, promotion into South West One West came and Newton were soon established at this level as one of the top sides in Devon again. Finishing second earned them a play-off at Reading, but this proved a match too far, and the home side won. Nevertheless, they were on an upward trend. The next season they went one better; this time another second place coupled with a better playing record earned a home play-off against High Wycombe, which Newton won.

Subsequently, and most recently with three successful years in National Three South and West under their belts the All Whites have now become one of the established clubs at this level. In 2012/13 they finished fourth, their best ever position. They also had the satisfaction of doing the double over each of the other Devon sides, Barnstaple, Brixham and Exmouth – who themselves finished in second place and were promoted after a play-off win.

On the playing side the club continues to strive for further improvement in a challenging league, aiming to follow their East Devon rivals into National South Two.

On a sadder note, the period since the club's centenary has naturally seen the passing of a number of the stalwarts of the club, some in particularly distressing circumstances. One was Barry Venning, who played most of his rugby at prop but occasionally in the back row who, like Bill Furze (see Chapter 13) died on the playing field. He had a heart attack whilst playing for Newton's Second XV against Teignmouth Seconds at Rackerhayes. An on-pitch attempt at resuscitation was made by Ken Lewis, who had been the referee for the earlier First XV game, and who had gained first-aid experience during his long service with the Royal Navy. Sadly his efforts were in vain.

Barry was probably ahead of his time; he had handling skills and loved to run with the ball, attributes more associated with modern players. His qualities earned him a place in the Devon side through the mid-sixties and for a while he played for Paignton.

As for his would be saviour, Ken went on to a varied career that took in teaching, tax-collector, local councillor and supporter at Rackerhayes where he still attends most First XV games.

Another loss was Roy Baker, who was arguably the 'Mr Rugby' of Newton Abbot for many years, serving as player, Captain and Club Secretary, the post he held when he died in hospital after a short illness. His playing career began in the early fifties and continued until 1967. He played either at prop or second-row and was one of the mainstays of the pack during one of the best post-war eras at the club. He was capped for Devon in 1963, captained the All Whites for six years in the sixties and served on the Devon committee for three seasons in the early seventies.

The recent sudden death of Duncan Christophers, at the age of 44 was probably the most poignant moment of recent times at the club. A popular sportsman, he was taken ill at the club's dinner and dance on 5 May 2012 and in spite of the best efforts of an army paramedic who was at the dinner, and ambulance and medical personnel, he died later in hospital. His funeral drew a massive congregation – estimated at 700 – to St Andrew's Church, Ashburton. It is unlikely that the Dartmoor Lodge Hotel has ever seen such a well-attended wake, as his family, friends and his many sporting acquaintances reminisced long into the evening. Duncan left a widow and two young children.

Duncan's rugby playing career began at Ashburton, and he then moved on to Buckfastleigh, Paignton and Brixham. He moved to Rackerhayes along with fly-half Richard Poustie, and both were influential in getting Newton out of Devon One and on the promotion path to their current status in National Three.

Duncan went on to captain the side for three seasons (2001-04) and by the time he retired from the First XV, the club was firmly established in the league structure and on the way up. The undoubted highlight of his career was lifting the Devon Senior Cup after the last gasp 33–31 win over Brixham at Astley Park on 25 April 2004.

He played almost exclusively in the second row, and was renowned as a hard but fair player, the sort of person you would prefer to have on your side than among the opposition. He was not only a very committed player but an inspiration to those around him.

The collection at Duncan's funeral realised some £3,250 for the Juniors Development Fund. A subsequent Memorial Game at the club raised further funds which have been used to create the Duncan Christophers Memorial Fund . The trustees will make grants to individual young sportsmen and women reflecting his wide sporting interests.

One of the biggest areas of expansion in rugby during the past forty years has been the creation of junior sections at many clubs, which encompass the age groups from Under 7 up to Under 16, after which players hopefully move up to Colts (Under 18) and/or the senior game.

The All Whites were one of the pioneers of junior rugby. Since the inception of their junior section, Newton have run teams across most age groups in nearly every season and have been a respected force across the county.

The club relies on a constant supply of coaches, referees and committee members to run the teams, but fortunately there are always willing volunteers coming forward. Over the years the RFU have devoted a lot of time and effort to supporting clubs in encouraging youth rugby. As a consequence coaches are themselves coached, referees are trained and child welfare officers are in place in every club with young players. Specific rules have been drawn up for the junior game, which sees a progression from tag rugby to contact on small pitches up to fifteen a side on full-sized pitches.

Each season Newton's Under 16s enter the Fisherman's Cup for clubs in the south of the county. The team has won the competition on four occasions, an achievement on a par with other participants. Devon RFU also run knock-out cups for the other fifteen-a-side age groups (Under 12 to Under 15), and again the Newton teams usually feature in the latter stages.

Festivals are organised for the 'mini' age groups, in which all the clubs come together at a host club for a day of pool and knock-out competition. Newton's youngsters always give a good account of themselves at these events.

The club's youth section consistently produces players capable of representing Devon, most recently two under 18 and one under 15 girls which in turn can lead to divisional recognition and ultimately England honours.

This policy and commitment to development over the years has resulted in a number of players going on to play representative rugby, but it is the inherent values and simple enjoyment of the game that has brought the most rewards. The sight of scores if not hundreds of muddy youngsters playing rugby and training every Sunday in the season makes it all worthwhile. It is quite possible to suppose that this dedication to youth rugby and raising standards has resulted in, not only the retention of youth players into adult rugby, but also in attracting players from the local area who relish the opportunity to play at a higher level or with an ambitious, well run, community based club.

Unfortunately a successful youth section does not guarantee a supply of players in senior rugby; retention of players is an ever-increasing problem, and a number of causes have been identified. The high fall-off rate is of concern to clubs and the RFU are always exploring initiatives to counter it, but thus far no sure fire solution has been found.

The club now boasts the most junior players it has ever had, plus ladies and girls teams. It is financially sound and was proudly the first team of its` level in the area to earn the coveted Rugby Football Union Accreditation Award. The RFU Club Accreditation scheme is based upon the six key drivers identified as crucial to a strong club; retaining & developing players, recruiting new players, recruiting & retaining high quality coaches, volunteers & referees, effective & efficient facilities, effective & efficient management and governance integration with the local community.

Each of these key drivers, together with the Core Values of the game, is represented within the Accreditation scheme and together they represent the component parts of a strong, sustainable club. The All Whites have already been re assessed and have passed with flying colours, a tribute to all those volunteers who give up so much time and energy for the good of the club.

The original management of the club by a few "jack of all trades" has been superseded over the years by a Board of Directors for the limited company, and a Club Executive which includes playing, commercial, communications and maintenance volunteer teams.

The junior element of the club now has its` own management team of parents and volunteers who are able to provide a positive rugby experience to hundreds of young people every weekend during the season.

Alongside these developments the club has been fortunate to benefit from the ongoing involvement of a number of families over several generations, plus the long term involvement of some individuals, for example the current Chairman Keith MacLean who played for the club over five decades!

One example of the innovation and drive that is necessary to keep the club afloat is the clubs` popular annual Event in the Tent, led by Phil Burford, which continues to raise money for the club, and its profile among businesses and public alike, by providing memorable evenings of entertainment involving visiting rugby VIPs and a social event par excellence.

Looking to the future the club waits eagerly for the 2015 Rugby World Cup, which, for the first time, sees games hosted at Sandy Park, just fifteen minutes up the road. The All Whites are delighted that four of its youngsters; Poppy Hannis-Smith, Georgia Scrase- Vallance, Jack Sweeney and Torrin Stone were one of the first groups of 2015 Young Rugby Ambassadors chosen by the RFU as part of its commitment to develop young volunteers throughout the game. We are sure they will do us proud.

So what happens next? The clubs long association with Rackerhayes is now under question. This proud old club is packed with players but is now showing its` age. Facilities, whilst lovingly patched up over the years, are now approaching the end of their useful life, particularly given the levels of rugby we now entertain, the growing number of children playing and the recent arrival of female players and officials. But further work and investment is only worth it in the longer term if it is to stay at its` current location.

The club does now boast disabled facilities, dedicated physiotherapy rooms and dedicated junior spaces for the first time, and, whilst grateful for the recent donations from the RFU and Landfill Community Funds through Ugbrooke Environmental Limited, which have made it possible, the club now looks to its' landlords, Sibelco, the successors to local clay company Watts Blake & Bearne, for its' longer term future, whether at Rackerhayes or elsewhere.

Watch this space, and here`s to the next 150 years!

Matches & Events 1990-2013

The Havill Plate Final

NEWTON ABBOT R.F.C.
1st XV
v.
WESSEX R.F.C.
1st XV

Sunday 28th April 1996 • Kick Off 3.00 p.m.

NEWTON ABBOT R.F.C.

15	W. THRESHER
14	K. GLOVER
13	M. BEAVIS (Capt.)
12	G. GARRETT
11	N. HOUGHTON
10	D. HERBERT
9	A. FOSTER
1	N. HAMMOND
2	S. DONNELLY
3	A. KINMOND
4	D. WHORTON
5	D. RAMSEY
6	C. LARGE
7	R. NARRAMORE
8	J. SAMPSON

Replacements from:

16	S. LOVEGROVE
17	P. HARVEY
18	P. DAVEY
19	R. BERE
20	J. BLACK
21	L. HUSBAND

Coach: C. MAHON

WESSEX R.F.C.

15	R. LAMBERT *
14	S. BOATFIELD
13	G. TOUCHINGS
12	J. CARPENTER *
11	P. HURFORD
10	L. THORPE *
9	G. CHUGG *
1	D. BOWEN
2	D. FURZER
3	B. LOUGHMAN *
4	S. FARMER
5	M. LYN
6	R. JENKINS
7	P. BYE * (Capt.)
8	R. MEARS *

Replacements:

16	P. GOODING
17	J. HAYMEN
18	D. MORRIS
19	T. EDMUNDS

Coaches: G. MELDON
S. BANKS

* County Representatives

Newton Abbot Rugby Football Club
WISH TO OFFER SPECIAL THANKS THIS WEEK TO

AD-POWER MAILING SERVICES

*Ad-Power Mailing Services wish both teams all the best
in this Havill Plate Final.*

Referee: T. Rice (D.R.R.S.)
Touch Judges:
Alan Meagor (D.R.R.S.), N. Powell (D.R.R.S.)

Medic in attendance
M. Rawle

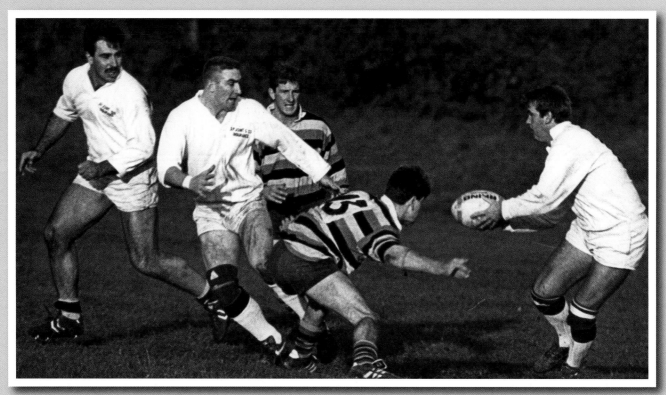

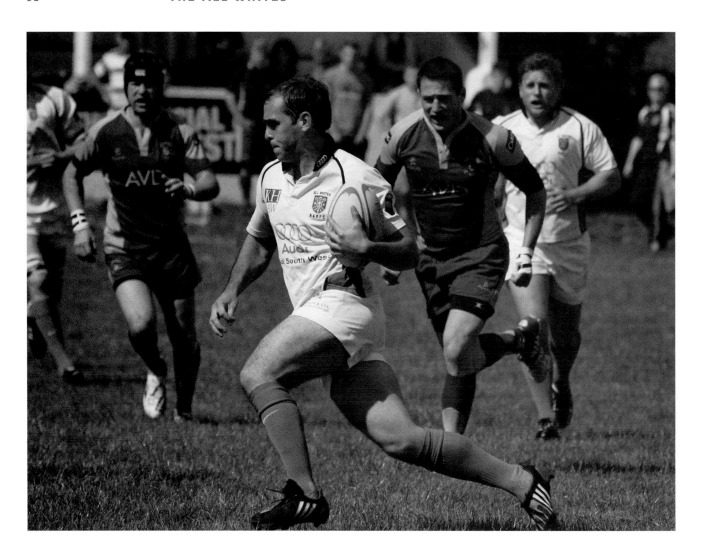

Duncan Christophers' Memorial

Juniors

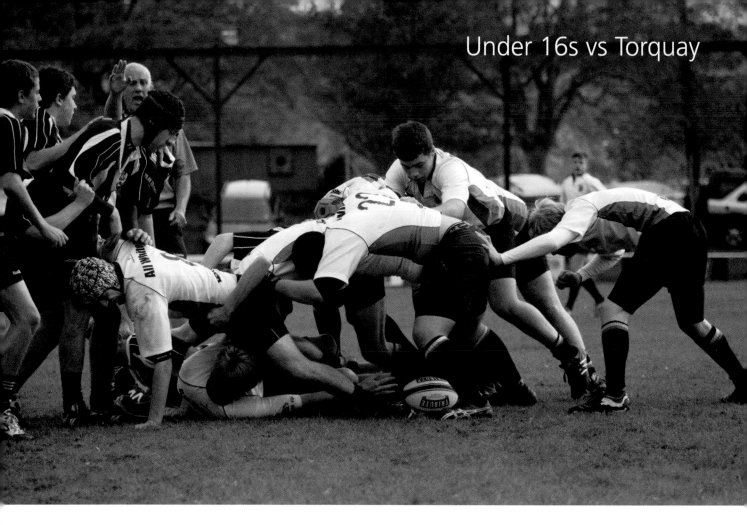

Under 16s Shield Final

Women's Rugby

APPENDIX I

Office Holders

Season	President	Chairman	Secretary	Treasurer
1888/9	Rev. G.T. Warner		W.H. James	H. Rodgers
1889/90	Mr Hardiman			
1890/1	Rev. G.T. Warner		T. Hayden	Mr Russell
1891/2			W. Dawe	Mr Roberts
1892/3				H. Rodgers
1893/4				
1894/5	W. Vicary		H. Rodgers	J. Taverner
1895/6	H. Knight		H. Rodgers	J. Taverner
1896/7				
1897/8				
1898/9	Dr E. Hunt		V. Judd	H. Knight
1899/1900	Dr E. Hunt		H. Rodgers	H. Knight
1900/01	W.M. Ball		H. Rodgers	H. Knight
1901/02	W.M. Ball		H. Rodgers	H. Knight
1902/03	W.M. Ball		H. Rogers	H. Knight
1903/04	W.M. Ball		H. Rodgers	H. Knight
1904/05	W.M. Ball		H. Rodgers	H. Knight
1905/06	W.M. Ball		F. Valley	H. Knight
1906/07			F. Valley	H. Knight
1907/08	R. de V. Whiteway Wilkinson			
1908/09	R. de V. Whiteway Wilkinson		R.S. Stephens	H.A. Phillips
1909/10	R. de V. Whiteway Wilkinson		R.S. Stephens	H.A. Phillips
1910/11	W.R.V. Webb		R.S. Stephens	W.A. Bond
1911/12	W.R.V. Webb		R.S. Stephens	W.A. Bond
1912/13	C.L. Vicary		R.S. Stephens	W.A. Bond
1913/14	B.D. Webster		R.S. Stephens	B. Reeve
1914/15	B.D. Webster		R.S. Stephens	B. Reeve
1919/20	B.D. Webster		R.S. Stephens	B. Reeve
1920/1	C.L. Vicary		R.S. Stephens	B. Reeve
1921/2	C.L. Vicary		R.S. Stephens	B. Reeve
1922/3	C.L. Vicary		R.S. Stephens	B. Reeve
1923/4	C.L. Vicary		R.S. Stephens	B. Reeve
1924/5	C.L. Vicary		R.S. Stephens	B. Reeve
1925/6	C.L. Vicary		R.S. Stephens	B. Reeve
1926/7	C.L. Vicary		R.S. Stephens	B. Reeve
1927/8	C.L. Vicary		R.S. Stephens	B. Reeve
1928/9	C.L. Vicary		R.S. Stephens	B. Reeve
1929/30	C.L. Vicary			B. Reeve
1930/1	C.L. Vicary		W.H. Edworthy	B. Reeve
1931/2	C.L. Vicary		R. Coombe	B. Reeve
1932/3	C.L. Vicary		R. Coombe	B. Reeve
1933/4	C.L. Vicary		E.E. Flood	B. Reeve
1934/5	C.L. Vicary		E.E. Flood	C.A. Jackson

Season	President	Chairman	Secretary	Treasurer
1935/6	C.L. Vicary		E.E. Flood	C.A. Jackson
1936/7	C.L. Vicary		E.E. Flood	C.A. Jackson
1937/8	C.L. Vicary		E.E. Flood	C.A. Jackson
1938/9	C.L. Vicary		E.E. Flood	C.A. Jackson
1939/40	C.L. Vicary	P. Hodge	E.E. Flood	C.A. Jackson
1946/7	J.C.H. Gibson		E.E. Flood	V.A. Pollard
				C.H. Harris
1947/8	J. Watts	H. Mills	E.E. Flood	C.H. Harris
1948/9	J. Watts		E.E. Flood	
			J.E. Evans	
1949/50	J. Watts	H. Mills	E.E. Flood	C.H. Harris
			J.E. Evans	
1950/1	J. Watts	H. Mills	E.E. Flood	H. Shobrook
			C.F. Frost	
1951/2	J. Watts		C. Frost	G. Bowden
1952/3	J. Watts			
1953/4	J. Watts			
1954/5	J. Watts	C. Harris	J.C. Nicholls	G. Bowden
			J.K. Poat	
1955/6	J. Watts	C. Harris	J.K. Poat	G. Bowden
1956/7	J. Watts	Major J. Evans	J.K. Poat	G. Bowden
1957/8	J. Watts	Major J. Evans	J.K. Poat	G. Bowden
1958/9	J. Watts	Major J. Evans	J.K. Poat	G. Bowden
1959/60	J. Watts	Major J. Evans	J.K. Poat	G. Bowden
1961/2	J. Watts	J. Brock	J.K. Poat	G. Bowden
1962/3	J. Watts	J. Brock	J.K. Poat	G. Bowden
1963/4	J. Watts	Major J. Evans	J.K. Poat	G. Bowden
1964/5	J. Watts	Major J. Evans	J.K. Poat	G. Bowden
1965/6	J. Watts	Major J. Evans	J.K. Poat	G. Bowden
1966/7	J. Watts	Major J. Evans	J.K. Poat	G. Bowden
1967/8	J. Watts	Major J. Evans	J.K. Poat	G. Bowden
1968/9	J. Watts	Major J. Evans	J.K. Poat	G. Bowden
1969/70	J. Watts	Major J. Evans	R. Baker	G. Bowden
1970/1	J. Watts	S. Ward	R. Baker	G. Bowden
1971/2	J. Watts	S. Ward	R. Baker	G. Bowden
1972/3	J. Watts	S. Ward	R. Baker	G. Bowden
1973/4	J. Watts	J. Nicholls	R. Baker	G. Bowden
1974/5	J. Watts	J. Nicholls	R. Baker	K. MacLean
1975/6	J. Watts	T. Yabsley	R. Baker	K. MacLean
1976/7	J. Watts	T. Yabsley	R. Baker	K. MacLean
1977/8	J. Watts	T. Yabsley	R. Baker	K. MacLean
1978/9	J. Watts	B. Loder	R. Baker	B. Frankes
1979/80	J. Watts	B. Loder	R. Baker	B. Frankes
1980/1	J. Watts	B. Loder	R. Baker	B. Frankes
1981/2	J. Watts	W. Rogers	R. Baker	A.G. Dawes
1982/3	J. Watts	W. Rogers	R. Baker	A.G. Dawes
1983/4	J. Watts	W. Rogers	R. Baker	A.G. Dawes
1984/5	J. Watts	J. Beddow	R. Baker	A.G. Dawes
1985/6	J. Watts	J. Beddow	R. Baker	A.G. Dawes
1986/7	J. Watts	J. Beddow	R. Baker	A.G. Dawes
1987/8	J. Watts	R. Burgin	R. Baker	A.G. Dawes

Season	President	Chairman	Secretary	Treasurer
1988/9	J. Watts	R. Burgin	R. Baker	A.G. Dawes
1989/90	J. Watts	R. Burgin	R. Baker	A.G. Dawes
1990/1	J. Watts	R. Burgin	R. Baker	A.G. Dawes
1991/2	B. Loder	Dr J. Kirk	G. Hooper	G. Rooke
1978/9	J. Watts	B. Loder	R. Baker	B. Frankes
1979/80	J. Watts	B. Loder	R. Baker	B. Frankes
1980/1	J. Watts	B. Loder	R. Baker	B. Frankes
1981/2	J. Watts	W. Rogers	R. Baker	A.G. Dawes
1982/3	J. Watts	W. Rogers	R. Baker	A.G. Dawes
1983/4	J. Watts	W. Rogers	R. Baker	A.G. Dawes
1984/5	J. Watts	J. Beddow	R. Baker	A.G. Dawes
1985/6	J. Watts	J. Beddow	R. Baker	A.G. Dawes
1986/7	J. Watts	J. Beddow	R. Baker	A.G. Dawes
1987/8	J. Watts	R. Burgin	R. Baker	A.G. Dawes
1988/9	J. Watts	R. Burgin	R. Baker	A.G. Dawes
1989/90	J. Watts	R. Burgin	R. Baker	A.G. Dawes
1990/1	J. Watts	R. Burgin	R. Baker	A.G. Dawes
1991/2	B. Loder	Dr J. Kirk	G. Hooper	G. Rooke
1992/3	B. Loder	Dr J. Kirk	M. Henderson	G. Rooke
1993/4	B. Loder	K. MacLean	S. Lock	G. Rooke
1994/5	Dr J. Kirk	K. MacLean	D. Hart	G. Rooke
1995/6	Dr J. Kirk	K. MacLean	M. Young	G. Rooke
1996/7	Dr J. Kirk	D. Hooper	M. Young	L. Young
1997/8	R. Shuttleworth	D. Hooper	M. Young	J. Penkin
1998/9	R. Shuttleworth	D. Hooper	M. Young	D. West
1999/2000	R. Shuttleworth	D. Hooper	M. Young	D. West
2000/01	R. Shuttleworth	D. Hooper	M. Young	D. West
2001/02	R. Shuttleworth	D. Hooper	M. Young	D. West
2002/03	I. Glendinning	D. Hooper	A. Blee	G. Marshall
2003/04	I. Glendinning	G. Rooke	Lt Col R. Elliott	A. Bowman
2004/05	I. Glendinning	G. Rooke	Lt Col R. Elliott	A. Bowman
2005/06	I. Glendinning	G. Rooke	Lt Col R. Elliott	D. West
2006/07	I. Glendinning	G. Rooke	Lt Col R. Elliott	D. West
2007/08	I. Glendinning	G. Rooke	Lt Col R. Elliott	D. West
2008/09	I. Glendinning	G. Rooke	Lt Col R. Elliott	A. Romain
2009/10	I. Glendinning	G. Rooke	M. Gibbs/A. Hart	A. Romain
2010/11	I. Glendinning	G. Rooke	A. Hart	A. Romain
2011/12	I. Glendinning	G. Rooke	A. Hart	A. Romain
2012/13	I. Glendinning	K. MacLean	M. Brooks	A. Romain
2013/14	G. Rooke	K. MacLean	M. Brooks	A. Romain

APPENDIX II

Merit Tie Recipients

The First Merit Tie Recipients

<u>Players</u>
R. Baker
D. Bennett
C. Bowen
N. Bunclark
H. Dart
D. Drake
W. Furze
D. Gilpin
A. Kennard
K. Lock
P. McCue
G. Mills
S.A. Morris
R. Mudge
G. Swillabeer
B. Thomas
C. Wakeham

<u>Members and Officials</u>
Dr D.J. Batterhoum
A. Bearne
A. Bickleigh
G. Bowden
R. Counter
F. Critchley
R. Daw
J. Dunford
Major J.E. Evans
W. Gray
H. Hingston
I. Hooper
R. Kilburn
S.R. Morris
J. Nicholls
R. Parker
J.K. Poat
H. Simmons
G. Tribble
L. Tucker
W.J.B. Watts

Later Recipients

2003-04
Paul Warren, Gary Lynch, Jenny Edgcumbe,
Mary Hooper

2004-05
Paul Dowrick, Richard Parker, Steve Bulman,
Darren Walton, Pete Evans

2005-06
Andrew Bullivant

2006-07
Bill Murphy, Andy Breeze, Adam Battams,
Marc Bayley,

2007-08
Phil Burford, Lee Sayer

2008-09
Simon Mabin, Tom Meek

2009-10
Ian Harvey, Russ Baker, Neil Johns, Steve Smith,
Richard England

2010-11
Alex Stentiford, Ray Elliott, Steve Joint

2011-12
Roy Bryant, Mike Brooks, Ian Milton, Mike Saxton,
Jason Keenan, Nic Holt, Alex Moore, Matt
Templeman

2012-13
Paul Sheffield, Gary Owen, Dan Marsh,
Jan Viskoper, Roy Jones

APPENDIX III

Winners of Club Awards

Chris Wakeham Trophy for the Playing Clubman of the Year

1970-71	Trevor Harvey
1971-72	John Greenwood
1972-73	Dave Aggett
1973-74	Tony Schafer
1974-75	Keith MacLean
1975-76	Alan Rogers
1976-77	Gordon Hooper
1977-78	Phil Husband
1978-79	Phil Loder
1979-80	Peter Horrell
1980-81	Ian Glendinning
1981-82	Keith Ellis
1982-83	Roger Medland
1983-84	Chris Aggett
1984-85	Rob Shaw
1985-86	Bruce Prowse
1986-87	Geoff Garrett
1987-88	Alan Baker
1988-89	Ron Strickland
1989-90	Mark Beavis
1990-91	Rob Narramore
1991-92	Nick Crout
1992-93	Tony Hart
1993-94	Stewart Cook
1994-95	Ashley Foster
1995-96	Brian Male
1996-97	Duncan Christophers
1997-98	Stuart Donnelly
1998-99	Graham Rees
1999-00	Roger Trant
2000-01	Digger Whorton
2001-02	Richard Beere
2002/03	Ian Harvey
2003-04	Tony Wolke
2004-05	Steve Gibbs
2005-06	Ian Barnes
2006-07	Devon Melville
2007-08	Jason Keenan
2008-09	Simon Mabin
2009-10	Nigel Cane
2010-11	Matt Templeman
2011-12	Andy Breeze
2012-13	Nic Holt

Neil Ashcroft Cup for the 2nd XV Player of the Year

2006/07	Declin Hammond
2007/08	Lee Williams
2008/09	Damien Milden
2009/10	Andy Breeze
2010/11	Tom Meek
2011/12	Aaron Page
2012/13	George Heath

Coaches' Cup for the non-1st XV Clubman of the Year

2012/13	Mike Way

Len Taylor Cup for the 1st XV Player of the Year

1982-83	Paul Hughes
1983-84	Phil Loder
1984-85	Royston Barnes
1985-86	Mark Beavis
1986-87	Richard Poustie
1987-88	Gary Kennard
1988-89	Roger Trant
1989-90	Richard Poustie
1990-91	Dean Lucas
1991-92	James Black
1992-93	Stewart Cook
1993-94	Rob Narramore
1994-95	Christian Longhurst
1995-96	Mark Beavis
1996-97	Digger Whorton
1997-98	Richard Poustie
1998-99	Harry Langley
1999-00	John Sampson
2000-01	Nick Southern
2001-02	Duncan Christophers
2002-03	Bill Murphy
2003-04	Duncan Christophers
2004-05	Ian Barnes
2005-06	Simon Mabin
2006-07	Jack Burford
2007-08	Duncan Christophers
2008-09	Jason Keenan
2009-10	Andy Birkett
2010-11	Nic Holt
2011-12	Jason Keenan
2012-13	Lloyd Radford

Glen Loder Shield for the Leading 1st XV Try Scorer

1986-87	Mark Beavis
1987-88	Paul Hughes & Roger Trant
1988-89	Andy Monnington
1989-90	Andy Monnington
1990-91	Andy Monnigton
1991-92	Andy Monnington
1992-93	Andy Monnington
1993-94	Andy Monnington
1994-95	Andy Monnington
1995-96	Karl Glover
1996-97	Karl Glover
1997-98	Karl Glover
1998-99	Steve Loder
1999-00	Steve Loder & Ian Coombes
2000-01	Allan Barkas
2001-02	Bill Murphy
2002-03	Bill Murphy
2003-04	Bill Murphy
2004-05	Kevin Francis
2005-06	Devon Melville
2006-07	Michael Louwrens
2007-08	Jan Viskoper
2008-09	Nic Holt
2009-10	Simon Mabin
2010-11	Thor Normann
2011-12	Pete Mortimore
2012-13	Eddie McGinley

Captain's Cup for Captain's Player of the Year

1998-99	Harry Langley
1999-00	Richard Beere
2000-01	Duncan Christophers
2001-02	Chris Van Der Merwe
2002-03	Paul Warren
2003-04	Keith MacLean
2004-05	Simon Mabin
2005-06	Jonathan Bourne
2006-07	Andy Breeze
2007-08	Simon Mabin
2008-09	Matt Templeman
2009-10	Mike Saxton
2010-11	Ben Cole
2011-12	Nic Holt
2012-13	Josh Smith

Chairman's Cup for the 3rd XV Player of the Tear

1997-98	Graham Rees
1998-99	Paul Jelly
1999-00	Pete Davey
2000-01	Andy Bullivant
2001-02	Steve Smith
2002-03	Tony Wolke
2003-04	Pete Evans
2004-05	Steve Adams
2005-06	Marc Bayley
2006-07	Marc Bayley
2007-08	Paul Sheffield
2008-09	Mark Shaddick
2009-10	Will Smith
2010-11	Nathan Messer
2011-12	Andy Breeze
2012-13	Gary Owen

President's Cup for the 2nd XV Player of the Year

1997-98	Ben Feasby
1998-99	Andy Brook
1999-00	Paul Warren
2000-01	Danny Costello
2001-03	Dave Herbert
2002-03	Adam Battams
2003-04	Richard Holyoak
2004-05	Steve Clements
2005-06	Adam Battams
2006-07	Steve Baker
2007-08	James Houghton
2008-09	Richard England
2009-10	Paul Hooper
2010-11	Jared Baker
2011-12	Josh Vickridge
2012-13	Aaron Page

Coach's Cup for the Player Showing the Most Skills

1993-94	Neil Houghton
1994-95	John Sampson
1995-96	Richard Beere
1996-97	
1997-98	Ian Schafer
1998-99	Ian Peacock
1999-00	Andrew Ash
2000-01	Jared Baker
2001-02	Jason Wescott
2002-03	Danny Vickridge
2003-04	Ian Barnes
2004-05	Simon Mabin

2005-06	Joe Frost
2006-07	Jonathan Bourne
2007-08	Rob Boles
2008-09	Andy Birkett
2009-10	Jason Keenan
2010-11	James Head
2011-12	Tom Channon
2012-13	Pete Mortimore

Coach's Cup for the Most Committed Player

1996-97	Nick Crout
1997-98	Chris Grice
1998-99	Andy Kinmond
1999-00	Nick Hammond
2000-01	Richard Beere
2001-02	Andy Kinmond
2002-03	Steve Smith
2003-04	Andy Breeze
2004-05	Paul Warren
2005-06	Duncan Christophers
2006-07	Paul Dowrick
2007-08	Alex Moore
2008-09	Neil Johns
2009-10	Matt Templeman
2010-11	Alex Jeffery
2011-12	Matt Templeman
2012-13	Alex Gale

Phil Burford Cup for the Colts Player Making the Most Impact in Senior Sides

2002-03	Stuart Tomlin
2003-04	Simon Mabin
2004-05	Russ Burford
2005-06	Jack Burford
2006-07	Joe Burford
2007-08	James Head
2008-09	Sam Wallace
2009-10	no award
2010-11	Jake Monnington
2011-12	Will Taverner
2012-13	Mike Edworthy

Director of Rugby Team Cup for the Most Consistent Team in the Senior Club

1997-98	1st XV
1998-99	1st XV
1999-00	Newton Abbot Ladies XV
2000-01	Colts XV
2001-02	Under 16's XV
2002-03	Colts XV
2003-04	1st XV
2004-05	Colts XV
2005-06	1st XV
2006-07	Colts XV
2007-08	3 rd XV
2008-09	1st XV
2009-10	1st XV
2010-11	1st XV & Ladies XV
2011-12	Colts XV
2012-13	1st XV

Terry Yabsley Memorial Trophy for the Non-Playing Clubman of the Year

1988-89	Chris Pomeroy
1989-90	Ivor Hooper
1990-91	Tim Yabsley
1991-92	Tony Schafer
1992-93	Sherrill Lock
1993-94	Charlie Mahon
1994-95	Graham Heath
1995-96	Gareth Thomas
1996-97	Gordon & Mary Hooper
1997-98	Darren West
1998-99	Roger Medland
1999-00	Phil & Gill Loder
2000-01	Chris Wannell
2001-02	Jenny Edgecombe
2002-03	Tom Guirk
2003-04	Phil Burford
2004-05	Gilmour Fox
2005-06	Phil Burford
2006-07	Maurice Young
2007-08	The Grainger Family
2008-09	Roy Jones
2009-10	Martin Carnell
2010-11	Jack Burford
2011-12	Mike Brooks
2012-13	Graham Rooke

Supporters' Player of the Year Shield

1998-99	Steve Loder
1998-00	John Sampson
2000-01	Richard Beere
2001-02	Duncan Christophers
2002-03	Richard Beere
2003-04	Ian Barnes
2004-05	Stuart Kingsley
2005-06	Devon Melville
2006-07	Neil Johns
2007-08	Jason Keenan
2008-09	Richard Beere
2009-10	Simon Mabin
2010-11	Ben Cole
2011-12	Josh Smith
2012-13	Josh Smith

Graham Rooke Award for the Newcomer Making the Most Impact, in Whatever Capacity

2004-05	Russ Baker
2004-05	Luke Eketone
2005-06	Devon Melville
2006-07	Dave Bending
2007-08	Matt Templeman
2008-09	Trevor Harris
2009-10	Brett Stroud
2010-11	Tom Channon
2011-12	Matt Newman
2012-13	Kevin Dennis

Shield for the Colt Playing the Most Games in a Season

1987-88	Matthew Schafer
1988-89	Matthew Robinson
1989-90	Nick Crout
1990-91	Andrew Pidwell
1991-92	Richard Kirk
1992-93	Neil Houghton
1993-94	Alex McLead
1995-96	Andrew Ash
1996-97	Adam Hooper
1997-98	Oliver Hart
1998-99	Oliver Hart
1999-00	Tristian Baker
2000-01	Dave Huggins
2002-03	James Clarke
2003-04	James Halse
2004-05	James Clarke
2005-06	Ian Milton

2006-07	Damiem Milden
2007-08	Joe Avery
2008-09	Josh Smith
2009-10	Dan Brown
2010-11	Rob Davis
2011-12	Mike Edworthy & Harry Laity
2012-13	Alex Davey

TAPPE Cup for the Colt Scoring the Most Tries

2006-07	Alex Pugh
2007-08	Luke Cavazzanna
2008-09	Martyn Palmer
2009-10	Martyn Palmer & Sam Garland
2010-11	Ashley Gibbons & Aaron Page
2011-12	Harry Laity
2012-13	Sam Pavey

Trophy for the Most Improved Colts Player

1979-80	C Gallaghan
1980-81	Steve Howarth
1981-82	Shaun Phillips
1982-83	John Pidwell
1983-84	Rich Poustie
1984-85	Andrew Monnington
1986-87	Jason Dorrow
1987-88	Adam Cornish
1988-89	Alex Gordon
1989-90	Stewart Cook
1990-91	James Baker & Lee Young
1991-92	Simon Gibbons
1992-93	Jamie Robinson
1993-94	Dan Costello
1995-96	Steve Clements
1996-97	Marco Madiera
1997-98	Kevin Millin
1998-99	Alex Stentiford
1999-00	Ben Ridgeway
2000-01	Giles Bristol
2002-03	Liam Gooding
2003-04	Tim Prowse
2004-05	Paul Hooper
2005-06	Ben Tuckett
2006-07	James Colclough
2007-08	Matt Bottoms
2008-09	Bruce Whiting
2009-10	Tom Edwards
2010-11	Harry Laity
2011-12	John Lacey
2012-13	Sam Harrison

Colts' Clubman of the Year Award

1999-00	Ollie Hart
2000-01	Andrew Shaw
2002-03	Jamie Halse
2003-04	James Aggett
2004-05	Jamie Halse
2005-06	Alex Pugh
2006-07	Ryan Maunder
2007-08	Joe Avery
2008-09	Nick Wadge
2009-10	Jake Andrews
2010-11	Luke Smith
2011-12	Luke Smith
2012-13	Alex Davey

Bill Furze Trophy for the Colts Player of the Year

1970-71	Doug Brown
1971-72	Mark Feasby
1972-73	Tim Yabsley
1973-04	Geoff Trout
1974-05	Ron Stickland
1975-76	Chris Courtaux
1979-80	Dave Rockey
1981-82	Matt Tompkins
1982-83	Keith Steer
1983-84	Mark Beavis
1998-99	Newton Mills
1999-00	Geoff Hill
2000-01	Lee Williams
2001-02	James Drew
2003-04	Dave Huggins
2004-05	Eddie Cribb
2005-06	Alex Pugh
2006-07	Steve Baker
2007-08	Joe Avery
2008-09	James Head
2009-10	James Colclough
2010-11	Sam Holmes
2011-12	Max Snowden
2012-13	Torrin Stone

A&A Cup for the Colts Players' Player of the Year

2004-05	Alex Pugh
2005-06	Ian Milton & Darren White
2006-07	Damien Milden
2007-08	Mike Walters
2008-09	Josh Vickridge
2009-10	Dayne Layton
2010-11	Ashley Gibbons
2011-12	Alex Davey
2012-13	Jack Mitchell

Most Improved Lady Player Award

2008-09	Emma Jones
2009-10	Abbet Carpenter
2010-11	Laura Shearer
2011-12	Holly Feller

Ladies' Coach's Cup

2009-10	Emma Manning & Emma Jones
2010-11	Laura Waddington
2011-12	Samantha Tiffany

Ladies' Players' Player

2009-10	Claire Corrick
2010-11	Laura Waddington
2011-12	Emma Jones

Best Lady Newcomer

2011/12	Kat Parker

APPENDIX IV

Representative Honours

County players 1998–2013 (1st cap only mentioned)

1998	Rob Narramore
1999	Harry Langley, Rob Narramore, Steve Loder
2000	Darren Evans, Duncan Christophers
2005	Paul Warren, Ian Barnes, Kevin Francis
2006	Nick Hammond, Russ Burford, Jack Burford, Jon Bourne, Devon Melville
2008	Dave Kimberley, Nic Holt, Chad Thorne, Jason Keenan, Ben Scott, Joe Burford
2009	Paul Dowrick, Alex Lloyd
2010	Jamie Tripconey, Paul Creek
2011	Dan Force, Ben Rogers
2012	Tom Channon, Lloyd Radford, Pete Mortimore, Baz Chapman. Rob Avery-Wright, Josh Smith
2013	Dean Avery, James Hannaford, Matt Dowrick

England Under 20s counties

Tom Channon v Scotland 2011
Rob Avery-Wright v Georgia 2013

England Under 19's

Will Carrick-Smith v Ireland 2011

England Colleges

Lloyd Radford (Capt) v Irish Exiles and Portugal u 19s 2011
Ben Scott v Wales, Irleland & Scotland 2004

English Students

Simon Morell v Wales & England 2003

England Under 18's

Ro Murray v Wales A 1998
Simon Mabin v Scotland, Scotland A, Wales, English Schools 2003
Joe Burford v Italy (Capt) Portugal 2007

England under 16's

Alan Miller v Wales, Portugal & Italy 1998
Joe Burford v Italy 2005
Alex Gale Capt v Scotland, Belgium & France

British Police

Nick Southern v New Zealand Police 2000
Ben Cole Capt Tours to Canada, Australia & Hong Kong
Nic Holt Tour to Hong Kong 2013

Malta

Kyle Mason

British Police

2000 Nick Southern
2009 Nic Holt
2010 Ben Cole

Navy

Marc Roberts, Kyle Mason, Damien Chambers, Gareth Evans

APPENDIX V

500 Board
(Players who have played 500 times for a senior side)

Cliff Bowen
Ken (Topsey) Lock
Roy Baker
George Wills
Alan Rogers
Phil Husband
Keith MacLean
Phil Loder
Rob Shaw
Ron Stickland
Geoff Garrett
Graham Rees

APPENDIX VI

Life Members, 2013

Major John Evans D.S.O
Ken Lock
Joyce Lock
Keith MacLean
Sam Ward
Tony Schafer
Sue MacLean
Graham Rooke
Gordon Hooper
Mary Hooper
Phil Loder
Phil Burford

APPENDIX VII
1st XV Playing Record, 1884–1935

Season	Played	Won	Drawn	Lost	For	Against
1884/5	12	5	3	4	4 goals, 17 tries	4 goals, 5 tries
1885/6	22	18	2	2	48 goals, 37 tries	3 goals, 4 tries
1887/8	16	10	4	2	12 goals, 29 tries	4 goals, 26 tries
1888/9	25	17	3	5	27 goals, 20 tries	5 goals, 4 tries
1889/90	21	12	3	6		
1891/2	23	10	3	10	7 goals, 23 tries	16 goals, 23 tries
1892/3	36	15	7	14		
1893/4	35	16	4	15	242	160
1895/6	31	10	3	18	70	154
1896/7	30	5	4	21	107	305
1897/8	31	12	3	16	126	233
1898/9	30	17	2	11	169	210
1900/1	36	16	3	14	236	240
1902/3	32	10	2	20	166	290
1903/4	34	12	6	16	173	233
1904/5	40	18	2	20	320	329
1905/6	34	20	3	11	366	177
1907/8	34	18	2	14	314	155
1908/9	36	27	2	7	503	148
1909/10	37	26	3	8	429	157
1910/11	35	22	3	10	312	148
1911/12	37	32	2	3	610	134
1912/13	33	21	4	8	359	153
1913/14	36	21	5	10	422	180
1918/19	9	3	3	3	28	41
1919/20	34	22	4	8	321	123
1920/1	41	22	8	11	272	196
1921/2	40	27	8	5	331	136
1922/3	41	31	3	7	481	165
1923/4	41	34	3	4	486	184
1924/5	39	28	2	9	482	206
1925/6	38	29	3	6	492	215
1926/7	44	26	7	11	506	262
1927/8	43	23	5	15	462	333
1928/9	40	21	1	18	419	246
1929/30	36	12	4	20	335	392
1930/1	40	16	2	22	278	358
1931/2	38	19	4	15	386	272
1932/3	38	23	9	6	377	180
1933/4	40	22	2	16	429	293
1934/5	35	17	4	14	293	237

APPENDIX VIII

Leading Points Scorers, 1946–73

Season	Player	Tries	Conversions	Penalties	Dropped Goals	Points
1958/9	M. Bowen	7	52	22	1	194
1957/8	M. Bowen	7	36	31	2	192
1967/8	R. White	3	38	31	0	178
1946/7	W. Sanders	14	40	14	1	168
1964/5	S. Morris	11	25	19	6	158
1959/60	M. Bowen	10	32	16	3	151
1965/6	M. Bowen	9	36	12	3	144
1966/7	R. White	1	40	19	1	143
1965/6	S. Morris	8	16	19	7	134
1949/50	G. Emmett	11	15	22	1	132
1968/9	G. Arscott	17	17	12	3	130
1970/1	R. Towell	0	28	24	0	128
1963/4	S. Morris	4	21	21	3	126
1971/2	T. Harvey	3	20	22	0	118
1965/6	M. Scott	37	0	0	0	111
1959/60	R. Wotton	32	4	0	0	104
1962/3	S. Morris	1	20	19	1	103